Who am I?

Why am I here?

What do I do Now?

William F Johnson

PO Box 3335

Broken Arrow, OK 74013

William F. Johnson

ISBN: 0165993109

ISBN-13:9780615993102

DEDICATION

We dedicate this book to our children, grandchildren, and their children with the faith that they will reach their God-given destiny.

PICK UP A FREE BOOK

http://aslanpress.com

ACKNOWLEDGMENTS

The author acknowledges the insight, wisdom, and guidance of my wife Rita who helped write the original material on which this book is based; Ron and Rebecca Bounds for their love and encouragement through the process of putting this book together, their review of the original material, and suggestions for improvement; Beth Wynn for her suggestions and editing; and Larry and Natalie Dautenhahn for their assistance in the development of the content and material provided in this book.

Table of Contents

Introduction

"You have great potential." Many of us have heard these words but do not realize the double meaning. We have the potential to do great things, but so far we have not lived up to that promise. Sadly, most never will.

Secular and Christian book stores are filled with self-help books. People look for a quick fix that will take them beyond their immediate circumstances into a wonderful future. In our microwave oven world, we want instant transformation. Conferences, both secular and spiritual, are full of people seeking the key that will instantly transform their dull lives into something meaningful. They get a glimpse of their potential, and then go home filled with ideas. "This time I will make it," they insist, only to be discouraged when the promised results fail to appear. After a while the excitement generated by the conference fades, and discouragement sets in, so they search for another leader, conference, or meeting to re-inspire. And so the cycle continues.

Mountain top experiences are great, but we live most of our lives in the valley. It has been said that we learn more from our failures than we do from our successes. I agree; in our failures we are more apt to realize our need for God and seek Him passionately. Jesus told us that in this world we will have trouble, but take heart, "I have overcome the world "[John 16:33] Realizing our potential is a process of overcoming the troubles of this world, and allowing those experiences to mold us into the image of Christ.

As we progress towards our destiny, we will be tested

by delay, fear, difficulties, and injustice.

These tests are God's way of strengthening us for the road ahead. God will not let us fail. If we miss His mark, we will get a new opportunity to repeat the test. Many are stuck in this test loop. They face the same battle over and over again. This book leads the reader through the process of moving beyond the tests to realize their full potential.

This book can be a tool to help the reader ace the tests and break through common barriers to the destiny for which they have been created. Like the GPS receiver on a car's dashboard, this book helps the reader identify his or her specific destination, provide the best route to take, and alert the driver to dangerous conditions ahead.

The book is divided into three parts. Part one will help you answer the question, "Who am I?" Part two will help you decide the question, "Why am I here?" Part three will provide you with the answer to the question, "What do I do now?"

W.F. (Bill) Johnson

Part 1 - Who Am I?

1.   Deep in the Heart

Deep down inside of most of us there lies a hidden desire which we keep stuffed away and are afraid to even think about, let alone attempt to achieve. We have so suppressed our desire that we often do not even remember that we ever had one. We bury these desires for a number of reasons: we convince ourselves that it is only a childish dream, we believe that it is too incredible to even consider, we are afraid to hope because we are afraid we will fail, and we do not want to be disappointed again, or people will laugh at us. So we stuff the dream, and convince ourselves it was mere foolishness to even hope.

You say to yourself, "Get a life and find a real career."

Our dream dims, and eventually dies. We shove it so deep that we totally forget about it and go on with our lives and never realize our God-given purpose. But that dream that has been abandoned may probably be the Lord calling you to His destiny.

God prepared our calling from the very beginning; therefore, He has probably been leading us all our lives. He has been trying to steer us toward our destiny. It is God who wants to give you the desires of your heart. He is the one who put them there originally. It could prove informative to look back at your life and see how the Lord has been steering you and what He has already accomplished in you.

It was World War II. Down in the vacant lot between our house and the corner, was a combat zone. There were trenches, hedge rows, and forts all constructed with great care by a seven year old at play. They were there to provide cover for make believe armies fighting against the invading forces. Make believe guns with cardboard bayonets served to protect us as we chased the enemy out of Hollywood, Illinois. It was working because no enemy had been seen around our town. When someone would ask what I wanted to be when I grew up, my answer was always the same, a soldier. My father had been a marine in WWI and walked with a limp from a bayonet wound in his right ankle. He had pictures and medals to look at and touch. I too would be a soldier, protect our world from its enemies, and be a hero with medals and pictures to show my kids.

In high school things began to change. When asked about my future, practicality began to win out. A guidance counselor recommended engineering. "That's where the jobs will be in the future." My parents agreed. So it was off to an inauspicious five years at engineering college, and a solid, but not fulfilling career in electronics.

My goals included positional authority, financial security, and broad recognition. After twenty years in the industry, I had achieved most of my goals, but was still not satisfied. There had to be something more. I had climbed the ladder of success and should have been satisfied. I had reached the top of the ladder, but then looked around saw nothing of eternal value. I still did not know what I wanted to be when I grew up. I was still searching for something that would be fulfilling.

As you realize where you have been, what God has been

doing in your life, and what He has been teaching you, you can better see the destiny for which you have been preparing.

Landmarks

> *Jeremiah 31:21 (NKJV) "Set up signposts, Make landmarks; Set your heart toward the highway, The way in which you went.*

In Jeremiah 31:21 the literal translation of the word "landmarks" means to pile up rocks or stones to make a landmark. After Joshua led the Hebrews across the Jordan River, the Lord commanded them to take rocks from the river and put them in a pile to commemorate that important event in their history.[1] Landmarks of our lives represent places we have been and experiences we have had which have affected our lives. As we look back on our lives and identify specific events that have affected our progress, we will find sign posts pointing us toward God's purpose for our lives.

What has God been doing in your life? Answering this question requires serious and objective analysis of your life up to now to see where the Lord has taken you. Realize that you have been on a spiritual journey, sometimes programmed by God and sometimes going your own way. You will want to identify landmarks that show where you have traveled.

Growing up in Illinois, our family rarely attended church, but spiritual things always had an attraction to me.

---

[1] Joshua 4:5

When my father passed away in his early fifties, I was a student at Georgia Tech in Atlanta. The pastor who officiated at the funeral was the only clergy we knew. He had been chaplain of my high school football team. As we discussed funeral arrangements, he asked about my father's relationship with God, "Was he prepared to go home to the Lord?" The pastor's question haunted me. We did not have a good answer at the time. Later I learned that my father had been confirmed in the Lutheran church but had drifted away from church attendance.

When the pastor asked question it was one of those landmark events in my life. Back at school with some friends we began to search for God. With a few friends, I attended some of the largest churches in Atlanta, always searching, but nothing seemed to click. On one occasion in St. Augustine, Florida, we attended the oldest Anglican Church in the nation. Somehow in all this searching I came up empty and began to seek more worldly activities.

The next landmark in my life came when I met Rita and we got married. Rita and our daughter Rhonda attended church regularly. One of my requirements for a wife was that she be a spiritual person. While recognizing the need for God in our family I was quick to delegate the responsibility to my wife while I handled the more basic needs of money, food, and shelter.

When our son, Kevin, was born and was to be baptized, I felt the need to also be baptized. As I look back today, it was only a mere formality, but something changed inwardly. Outwardly my career and recreation remained unchanged. As a result our married life became stressed until Rita began attending a Bible study class. She told me it was a self-improvement class. One day I asked her, "If you are taking this self-improvement class, why do I feel like I am changing." The class, "Renewing Love," by Jo Anderson, taught Rita how to love me, and let God change me. The Lord then began to bring about a radical change in my life.

The next milestone event occurred in 1974. At the altar of a small church on the Mississippi gulf coast I admitted to myself and to God that I no longer could live without Him in my life. At that point I turned my life, my career, my family, and my future over to Him. Rita and I began to make decisions after long, searching prayer. The next thing we knew we had moved to San Diego and had begun to grow in leaps and bounds in an exciting church.

It was in the mountains of Southern California, near the town of Julian, that the Lord called me into full time ministry. He had begun preparing me long before He called me. My secular employment required me to start up several new organizations, which helped me in later as a church planter. My company also developed technical and management materials which gave me good experience in researching, writing and teaching on a variety of technical subjects. We traveled extensively teaching classes and presenting at conferences throughout the world. All of these experiences provided a basis for teaching and preaching in a church setting.

Activity

On a separate sheet of paper, draw your spiritual time line highlighting experiences when you felt exceptionally close to God, when you heard from Him, and the times you felt that you had a particular sense of His power. List the period and the event. It may be helpful to find someone with whom you can share your spiritual walk. It is important to speak aloud to another person; it seals it.

2.   Where have I been?

The things that happen in your life, good and bad, may be training you for the work for which God created you. I am not saying that God caused you to experience a great trauma, but God can use those experiences for His purposes. People who have suffered violence or serious illness are equipped to help others through similar issues.[2] Joseph's brothers sold him into slavery; later he was falsely accused and thrown into prison. Then he was able to save Egypt from a disastrous famine and at the same time save his brothers and family. [3] Experiences are some of the sign posts which point to your destiny.

Often as we pray and seek the Lord, He will give us direction. My experience has usually been that He will just give us the next right step to take, but not give us our final destination. If He showed us our future destiny, we might have two separate and distinct reactions. We might run ahead of Him and try to achieve it in our own strength and not wait for His timing. Our other reaction might be to disbelieve Him and think it is impossible, so we do nothing. His word is a lamp unto our feet which shows us the path, not a spotlight on the future destination.[4]

In addition, the Lord may use others to encourage us and point us to His purpose. Friends, parents, teachers, and pastors may recognize gifts and graces in us and give us advice for our future calling.

---

[2] Romans 8:28
[3] Genesis 50:20
[4] Psalm 119:105

In addition, persons with revelatory gifting may hear from God on our behalf and share this with us.

Amos 3:7 (NIV) Surely the Sovereign LORD does nothing without revealing his plan to his servants the prophets.

While encouragement from people who know us well and prophetic words may help to guide us to our destiny, these words must be tested[5] and confirmed before we run off chasing their words about our future.

With a big smile on his face, the young Latino in the wheel chair pushed his way into the kitchen and up to the dining table. As he introduced himself to the men's fellowship group of the North Claremont United Methodist Church in San Diego, we realized he was going to be our morning speaker. Jose' had recently graduated from Berea Bible College where he had met a member of our church who also studied at Berea. Several years earlier, Jose', a Mexican National from Tecate, had been in a serious automobile accident while working in the U.S. which left him paralyzed from his waist down. He believed that God had saved him from death for a purpose. As a result he turned to God in a big way. Someone had given him a beat up old Chrysler and had installed equipment which enabled him to drive all over Mexico sharing Jesus and teaching the Gospel where ever he went. He was truly an evangelist. At the Men's meeting, Jose' shared his dream with all the men present.

The new president of Mexico, Luis Echeverría, had reinstituted an old land reform policy, which allowed

---

[5] 1 Thess 5:20

settlers to occupy and improve land for two years after which time they could claim ownership. Literally thousands of peasants could now have a place of their own.

Jose's dream was to plant churches in these settlements. His first one would be fifteen kilometers south of Tecate in a valley called Sierra Azul. He asked if our group would help with funding, materials, and physical labor in building the church facility. We were excited and quickly agreed.

The next Saturday, a caravan of pickup trucks loaded with tools and building material pulled up at the U.S. border crossing near Tecate. After a check of papers, all but one of us were waved through. Mr. Mihn, a refugee from Viet Nam, was turned back because he lacked proper papers. Getting into Mexico with all of our stuff was more difficult. We had to convince the authorities that we were not going to sell material that would require a tariff. After buying the appropriate insurance, we proceeded to Sierra Azul where several hundred people now lived in huts made of whatever anyone could find. Mostly they used cast off aluminum signs for a roof with mud and clay for walls and floors. Some would just dig a hole in the ground for a place to sleep. New settlers were constantly arriving.

A group had begun a business of making adobe bricks the ancient way by digging and casting the bricks by hand, then drying them by stacking them up in a dome shape around a wood bonfire. Our electrical tools for constructing the building were useless as the nearest electrical outlet was fifteen kilometers away.

The chief architect for the city of Tecate had been led to Christ at one of Jose's meetings. He kept his job with the city but became the pastor of the Sierra Azul. He taught us how to build the old fashioned way, without power tools or any modern convenience. For a level we used a clear plastic garden hose filled with water. Eventually we purchased a generator which would later be used to supply electricity for

the church, but we used to power our saws and tools. At the end of the summer our work was completed. The church held its first service in a packed building. This was my first experience at starting a new church from the ground up.

Two weeks before the first service was to be held, Jose' asked if I would go with him on a special trip. He was mysterious about where we were going and what we would do. With my friend Russ Loehr driving his pick up and me riding shotgun, we followed Jose's banged up old Chrysler back up Ensenada/Tecate Highway to Tecate. Arriving there we turned right on Route 2 towards Mexicali and drove about ten kilometers to a unpaved path leading north into the hills. This path appeared to be a deer trail. Looking back on it now it was probably a trail where undocumented workers crossed into the United States. We now realized how Jose's car developed its characteristic dents and scratches. We circled around rocks larger than our pick up and crossed small streams. The trip from the highway had lasted nearly a half an hour when Jose' stopped and signaled us to get out. We were on a rock strewn plateau with only a few scattered small trees and a lot of underbrush. The afternoon sun was bright and lit the entire plateaus with an orangish glow. Just the four of us, Russ, Jose', Jose's attendant and I were standing in a virgin wilderness. It felt very holy.

"This is where we are going to build the next church

building," Jose stated. "Today we are going to dedicate this site to the Lord." We walked around the area Jose had designated while we waited for others that Jose' had indicated would be coming.

By late afternoon about twenty people had gathered. After some introductions and fellowship, the dedication service began. Jose offered a prayer in Spanish, and then repeated it in English for our benefit. He then informed me that I was to give a message to the church people. Since I did not speak Spanish and they did not speak English only Jose knows whether they heard my message or one Jose translated. Then it was time to consecrate the land and pray for each of the people. Laying hands on them we prayed a blessing, as the Holy Spirit led our prayers. As I laid hands on one young man, the Spirit told me that he was to be the pastor of the church. Looking to Jose' for confirmation, he nodded and said that the young man was in seminary and would lead the church.

The entire plateau took on a new glow as the sun dropped behind the mountain giving the entire area a calmness and peacefulness that only comes from the Lord. We felt His presence and did not want to leave. This indeed was holy ground.

While we have never returned to that spot. I believe that was the beginning of God calling me to evangelism and to plant new churches. This was a sign post in my life pointing me to my future in ministry and God's call on my life.

> *Jeremiah 31:21 (NKJV) "Set up signposts, Make landmarks; Set your heart toward the highway, The way in which you went.*

The Lord, through the prophet Jeremiah, tells us we are to set up sign posts. Sign posts are things that show us how to get where we are going. This scripture says that we are to remember where we have been and find out where we are going and to stay on the road to our destiny.

Another skill required in ministry is the ability to communicate clearly. Looking back on my life, it is apparent that the Lord has been teaching me to communicate. Always fearful of public speaking, the Lord continuously put me in places and situations where it was impossible not to speak up. Writing came much easier. In the fourth grade, I wrote and produced a class play; in high school and college, I wrote and edited student newspapers; as an electronics engineer, I was published in trade journals and symposia. Then, for ten years as a director of a consulting firm, much of my time was spent writing proposals, training plans, manuals, and other publications. Having learned how to communicate, the Lord then called me to communicate the good news of the Kingdom of God.

Activity

<u>List the signposts in your life</u>

- What has God been saying to you?
- In your quiet time?
- In your dreams?
- Through prophetic words from others?
- From trusted friends and spiritual leaders?
- What has He been teaching you?
- What unique experiences has He taken you through or allowed you to experience?
- What lessons have you learned through failure?
- What training have you gone through, that you

did not consider being spiritual?

- How has God been preparing you?

3.   Knowing God

In our attempt to know who we are, we must first know God and understand our relationship with Him. The Holy Trinity unfolds to us; the Father's gift of love, Jesus' gift of life and the Holy Spirit's gift of power. We were created by God and He is the one who holds our destiny in His hands.

C. S. Lewis writes in *Mere Christianity*,

> *Your real, new self (which is Christ's and also yours, and yours just because it is His) will not come as long as you are looking for it. It will come when you are looking for Him.*

If we are to realize the purpose for which we were created we must understand our selves, but most importantly, we must have knowledge of God; that is have a close, intimate relationship with Him. The prophet Hosea communicated God's word to the nation of Israel in the days when they had become comfortable with their physical lives and felt they did not need God. They did all of the ritualistic things their religion required: sacrifices, giving of tithes, and attending temple services, but they did not know God.

> **Hosea 4:1 (NKJV)** [1] *Hear the word of the LORD, You children of Israel, For the LORD brings a charge against the inhabitants of the land: "There is no truth or mercy Or knowledge of God in the land."*

The Lord indicts the nation because they have lost truth; nothing is true, and everything is relative. They have forgotten mercy and "there is no knowledge of God in the land." The word "knowledge" translated is "Da ath" in

Hebrew. It is the same term used to describe an intimate relationship.

Adam "Da ath" Eve and they conceived a child. The Lord is saying that the people have no close, intense, intimate, emotional relationship with God. This does not mean there is no awareness of God - people may know about God, but there is no inner attachment to God. God wants a whole person relationship with us.

> **Mark 12:30** *Love the Lord your God with all your heart and with all your soul and with all your mind and with all your strength.'*

God's desire for Israel, and us, is spelled out in Hosea 6:6:

> *For I desire mercy and not sacrifice, And the knowledge of God more than burnt offerings.*

What God wants from us is an inner dedication, not just routine ceremony.

> *John 14:7 (NKJV)* ⁷ *"If you had known Me, you would have known My Father also; and from now on you know Him and have seen Him."*

God wants us to have a concern for His person, not just obedience to His commandments. The loss of "da-ath Elohim" is the real undoing of Israel and it is the undoing of the USA. In this country it is politically incorrect to love God with our whole being. It may be alright to read about God, but do not become a fanatic.

As a result of not having truth, mercy and knowledge of God, the Lord continues:

> **Hosea 4:2-4 (NKJV)** ²*By swearing and lying,*

> *Killing and stealing and committing adultery, They break all restraint, With bloodshed upon bloodshed. [3]Therefore the land will mourn; And everyone who dwells there will waste away With the beasts of the field And the birds of the air; Even the fish of the sea will be taken away. [4] Now let no man contend, or rebuke another; For your people are like those who contend with the priest.*

In his book "The Forgotten Father" Thomas Smail[6] writes that much of the church has forgotten God, the Father, and focused on the other two persons of the Trinity. Charismatics tend to focus on the Holy Spirit while evangelicals and some mainline denominations focus primarily on Jesus. Jesus taught us to know God, the Father, and how to pray to "our Father in heaven." An understanding of God the Father is important to our realizing our destiny.

> *"Abba is not Hebrew, the language of liturgy, but Aramaic, the language of home and everyday life ... We need to be wary of the suggestion ... that the correct translation of Abba is 'Daddy.' Abba is the intimate word of a family circle where that obedient reverence was at the heart of the relationship, whereas Daddy is the familiar word of a family circle from which all thoughts of reverence and obedience have largely disappeared ... The best English translation of Abba is simply 'Dear Father.'"[7]*

Without knowing God as our Father we do not understand God at all.

---

[6] Smail, Thomas A, *The Forgotten Father*,
[7] Smail, Thomas A, *The Forgotten Father*

J. I. Packer writes. [8]

"You sum up the whole of New Testament religion if you describe it as the knowledge of God as one's Holy Father. If you want to judge how well a person understands Christianity, find out how much he makes of the thought of being God's child, and having God as His Father. If this is not the thought that prompts and controls his worship and prayers and his whole outlook on life, it means he does not understand Christianity very well at all. For everything that Christ taught, everything that makes the New Testament new...is summed up in the knowledge of the Fatherhood of God. Father is the Christian name for God."

---

[8] Packer, J.I. *Knowing God*, p. 201.

The problem is we do not understand the meaning of Father. We live in a fatherless society. Nearly fifty percent of children sleep in a home in which their father does not live. Before they are eighteen, most of the children in the United States will spend a significant amount of time living separate from their father. Some fathers have abandoned the family physically through divorce, separation, or job location. Even when there is not physical separation - there is emotional separation.

Many children have poor relationships with their fathers because of the father's work schedules, alcoholism, drug abuse or the father is just absorbed in his own problems. This has been typical since the end of World War Two. Many of us grew up in families where our fathers were too busy for us. Many children were rejected, ignored or were never able to live up to the expectations of their fathers. Often fathers did not know how to be fathers.

As we have ministered in prisons throughout the country we have found that a majority of those incarcerated did not have a relationship with their fathers. In our fathers we find identity, value, abilities, and an understanding of our purpose in life. A strong father figure will give a child confidence and an understanding of who we are and an idea of our destiny. Tiger Woods, Michael Jordan, Wayne Gretzky, Pete Maravetch, John Maxwell, and others are all examples of a father's strong influence in the success of their children. Sometimes that influence leads in right directions and at other times not. But the strong father's influence provides identity, values, and confidence in the son or daughter.

Today there are adults and children who are searching

to find something to fill the emptiness left by the lack of knowing their father's love. Without the confidence of knowing our father's love, we become fearful, and lack confidence; so we play it safe, we are terrified of failing or making a mistake, living with the fear of rejection or failure. We compete with others to prove we are lovable. We keep trying to earn the father's love, but we never can measure up because of our need. As a result we go through life in fear - trying to protect what we have and bound up in trying to earn God's love. Some of us get by and are reasonably effective, but it is difficult for us to trust God. We trust Him for salvation, but we are afraid to trust him with our daily stuff. As a result we miss the abundant life He has in store for us. Cultural fatherless-ness leads to prodigal lifestyles. Sex, drugs, and rock and roll lead to more emptiness and the reawakened desire to find our father. In addition to losing fathers, we are losing the whole idea of fatherhood.

God, The Father, is the Christian Gospel. If we fail to see God as our father, we fail to realize the touch of His love that we are so desperately seeking.

> *The deepest search in life, it seemed to me, the thing that in one way or another was central to all living was man's search to find a father, not merely the father of his flesh, not merely the lost father of his youth, but the image of strength and wisdom external to his need and superior to his hunger, to which belief and power of his own life could be united. We may experience the Holy Spirit, but fail to realize the involvement of the Father. [Thomas Wolfe][9]*

Ultimately there is nothing in the world that can take the

---

[9] Thomas Wolfe

place of the Father's love; our pursuit leaves us empty. When we accept Jesus as our Savior, we need to remind ourselves that Jesus wants to introduce us to His Father.

We are all seeking love. We look first to our parents, especially our fathers. If we get the love we are looking for, then our tanks are filled. If not, we go through life trying to find this love in other relationships. However, the original father emptiness remains.

> *John 5:19-20 (NKJV)* [19] *Then Jesus answered and said to them, "Most assuredly, I say to you, the Son can do nothing of Himself, but what He sees the Father do; for whatever He does, the Son also does in like manner.* [20] *For the Father loves the Son, and shows Him all things that He Himself does; and He will show Him greater works than these, that you may marvel.*

Jesus states, "For the Father loves the Son....." The word translated in this passage is not "Agape" love, but "Phileo" love. Phileo is a word which describes the experience of love. Where "Agape" love is God's unconditional love toward us. "Agape" usually describes God's loving transactions from a distance.

> *"But God demonstrates his own love ["Agape"] for us in this: While we were still sinners, Christ died for us." [Romans 5:8(NKJV)]*

But when the Bible describes God's love coming close to us and actually touching our hearts, the word used is "Phileo." Phileo is distinguished from agape in that phileo more nearly represents tender affection. Jesus had a relationship with his father in heaven where He experienced this natural affection. In Mark 1:9-11 Jesus came from

Nazareth in Galilee and was baptized by John in the Jordan River. Coming up out of the water, they saw heaven being torn open and the Spirit descending on Jesus like a dove. God the Father spoke from heaven and said, "You are my Son, whom I love; [Phileo] with you I am well pleased." That's my boy! The Father gave the reassurance that Jesus' human heart needed.

The three most powerful words in the English language are "I Love You!" If we hear them from our father when we are young, they have a powerful affect for good. If we do not, the insecurities which result can undermine our success in life. Jesus heard those words and his heart was secure. "Yes! I am my father's son. He loves me." When Satan tried to derail Jesus from His mission he tried to get Jesus to prove His Sonship. Jesus did not have to prove himself by turning stones into bread; He relied on every word that His Father spoke. He knew He did not have to prove He was worthy of love. He knew He was the beloved of God, the one on whom God's favor rests.

So many of us feel we have to prove that we are loved. The enemy tempts us to do things to prove our self worth. To avoid the temptation, we need the experience that Jesus had: an experience of the demonstrated love that secures our hearts. Jesus was never far from His father. As we face the challenges of life, we also need to be sensitive to the voice of God our Father. Listening to the Father requires a heart secured by the same words that Jesus heard, "I love you!"

Jesus heard the same voice on the Mount of Transfiguration and in the Garden of Gethsemane. He knew the love from God the Father.

On His last night with His disciples Jesus told them He would be gone. How could they ever carry on without Him?

They knew Jesus had this relationship with His Father, but what would they do?

> *John 16:26-27 (NKJV) In that day you will ask in My name, and I do not say to you that I shall pray the Father for you; for the Father Himself loves you, because you have loved Me, and have believed that I came forth from God.*

We have direct access to the Father when we come in His name. Even more astounding is that when we love Jesus we can receive the love of His father. That "Phileo" love, the same demonstrated natural affection that Jesus experienced from the Father is available to everyone who places his faith in Jesus. When we really know the Father's love for us then we can break free of the need to prove ourselves. We can be free to try anything He asks us without the fear of failure, without the fear of rejection.

Jesus prayed for us

> *John 17:25-26 (NKJV) O righteous Father! The world has not known You, but I have known You; and these have known that You sent Me. And I have declared to them Your name, and will declare it, that the love with which You loved Me may be in them, and I in them."*

If we understand and experience the Love of God the Father our lives are transformed. When we get it deep down in our hearts it will change our lives. We have Identity - we are children of the living God. We have Value - our value

was placed on us by what the Father paid for us, His only begotten Son. We have confidence because we do not have to prove that we are lovable and we can afford to take risks and fail. Therefore, failure does not make us bad people and we can begin to understand why we are here. We know that God has a purpose for our lives.

Knowing The Father's, love is a problem of perception. The common fallacy is to equate the fatherhood of one's earthly father with an accurate representation of God's heavenly Fatherhood. Though not intentionally, or even consciously, we draw this equal sign in our mistaken equation at a deep subconscious level early in life.[10] Our first perceptions of what a father is like come from observation of our earthly fathers. God gave us earthly fathers. They were supposed to give their children an accurate picture of what a father should be. This would prepare children to understand God's Fatherhood as they grew up. However, sin came into the mix and messed it all up. Fathers do not do a very good job of showing us God's nature. If earthly fathers are intended to be mirrors, reflecting back some image of God, there is no denying the image is cracked and broken. The image they reflect is distorted.[11]

Our perception of our heavenly Father will often result from how we perceive our earthly father. Deeply imbedded broken images of fatherhood present some of the most serious barriers to the knowledge and experience of the Father's love.

Jesus points out that our earthly fathers are not perfect.

> *Luke 11:11-13 (NKJV) if a son asks for bread from any father among you, will he give him a stone? Or if he asks for a fish, will he give him a serpent instead of a*

---

[10] Michael Phillips, *A God to Call Father*

[11] Michael Phillips, *A God to Call Father*

fish? 12 Or if he asks for an egg, will he offer him a scorpion? If you then, being evil, know how to give good gifts to your children, how much more will your heavenly Father give the Holy Spirit to those who ask Him?"

Natural fathers are evil. The Greek word evil means harmful, injurious, etc. The devil wants to use this flaw in fathers. He does not want anyone to know the fullness of the Father's love. Through our natural father's distortions, the devil creates lies about the true nature of God the Father, and especially about His love for us. As in all things, sin interrupted and corrupted the process. The enemy has gone to great lengths to infiltrate the family unit, to discredit the earthly symbol of God's establishing. Instead of pointing us to God our Father, the incompleteness of earthly fatherhood has, with Satan's help, embittered sons and daughters against their parents and, in doing so, blinded them to the magnificence of God's Fatherhood. A gigantic stone sits in the middle of the road preventing each one of us from even thinking clearly, on the subject, let alone getting past the obstacle.[12] These stones are more than psychological misperceptions, they are spiritual strongholds.

There are many common distortions of our understanding of "father."[13]

"I have difficulty praying the Lord's Prayer because whenever I say 'Our Father' I think of my own father who was hard, unyielding, and relentless. I cannot help but think of God that way." [Martin Luther]

---

[12] Michael Phillips, *A God to Call Father*
[13] From Ed Piorek's book, *The Father Loves You*

The following categories are rather simplistic and few fathers would fall into a single category. More often, there will be combinations of all each. But, it is useful to look at some typical distortions of the father image of God.

Many have known their earthly father as the "Performance-Oriented Father." This is a common father type; he gives love based upon the performance of the child. Acceptance, affirmation, and affection are attached to achievement such as chores, education, sports, etc. Love is given or withdrawn in relation to the child's success. It comes in a variety of forms such as pushing the child to pursue a certain career, or requiring a certain dress code. The proverbial carrot is held out and usually carries on into adulthood. There is a time for rewarding achievement, but unconditional love and acceptance should not be based upon performance.

Sadly, the average man today has learned legalism instead of mercy from his earthly father. "Do what I say and I will love you," he has essentially heard growing up. "Disobey or make a mistake and I will not love you." He has not seen his father model mercy either by forgiving his son's mistakes or by asking his son to forgive his own mistakes. Thus the son grows up fearing failure, equating it with losing relationship with his father.[i]

Christians with this type of father perceive the Father in heaven as one who requires good performance in order to give the reward of love. A deep fear of failure drives him into religious striving.

Another common distortion of father is the Passive father. The passive father does not actively demonstrate love to his child. He does not speak words of love, nor offer an affectionate physical touch of love. As a result the developing child is deprived of emotional nourishment. Fathers in this category were either not at home much or they never demonstrated love. Fathers who traveled constantly, workaholics, alcoholics, or emotionally stoic people make up this category. Fathers can also be separated from their children through divorce or death. In these cases the need for a father cannot be met.

The resultant perception of God the Father is that he is distant, uninvolved, and undemonstrative. People with passive fathers often have difficulty in getting in touch with their emotions. It produces a sense of abandonment in the child. This causes the child to feel alone. Feeling alone and separated from the father's love is a painful experience. A father's sharp slap in the face causes a sharp pain that resides on the surface. A father's silence produces a dull wound: equally painful, but harder to identify. Abandonment can also produce a false sense of guilt in children. They blame themselves for their father's absence. This compounds their difficulty in experiencing the Father's love. Not only is God distant, but He sees them with some kind of disfigure-ment in their lives.

Anger over the unfairness of it all builds over time, and often an explosion of emotions reveals this latent father issue, allowing healing to begin.

The punitive father gives some form of abusive pain instead of love. This may be verbal, physical, or sexual abuse.

Victims of abuse often perceive God the Father as stern, harsh, punitive, unforgiving, and certainly unloving. Fear, shame, and anger are common emotional strongholds. Often these children love their father so much they cannot see the sin in their earthly fathers. These broken people desperately need the tenderness of the Father's love to enfold their fragile lives.

Most fathers have good qualities mixed with less desirable ones. There are no perfect fathers due to original sin. Everyone has to deal with some distortion. The challenge is to move beyond the good relationship they have with their earthly fathers, and in the spiritual sense to really give themselves to their Heavenly Father, trusting fully in Him for the deepest sort of love.

We often go through most of our lives before we begin to address our father issues. Why does it take so long? The pain was so deeply imbedded. We usually deal with everything else until we are forced to deal with the foundational issues. When we begin to deal with the father issues in our lives we enter a process of removing the broken lenses in order to see the Father as He really is.

- Acknowledge that we have a faulty image of "Father."

We have strong denial mechanisms. Recognizing that our father failed us makes us come face to face with the imperfections of his love. Allowing ourselves to feel unloved by our fathers is an experience we will usually avoid at all costs.

- Identify our specific faulty image

Identification reveals the areas where our natural father failed to reveal God's true nature.

- Remove our specific faulty image

Removal of faulty images requires us to forgive. To misrepresent God is to sin against the child. We must forgive our fathers for their sins against us. We do this primarily through prayer. We come to our heavenly Father and forgive our earthly fathers in Jesus' name.

As we forgive our earthly father, our heavenly Father reaches down and takes the distorted glasses from our eyes so we can see Him clearly. He touches the pain of our childhood and heals our wounded-ness. Forgiving our father should not be confused with blaming our father. We cannot hold them responsible for every difficulty we have experienced. We are responsible for our reactions to the problems. We have made bad choices in our attempt to find love and happiness in our lives. Children are to honor their fathers and mothers.

> *Exodus 20:12 (NKJV) "Honor your father and your mother, that your days may be long upon the land which the Lord your God is giving you.*
>
> *Ephesians 6:2-3 (NKJV) "Honor your father and mother," which is the first commandment with promise: 3 "that it may be well with you and you may live long on the earth."*

We are to maintain a posture of respect and love while we work through these issues with God. To deal with these issues we have to leave behind our bitterness and estrangement and move towards reconciliation with our fathers. Forgiving our father frees us from bitterness and releases us in other ways too. We no longer have to wait for our fathers to come to us and right the wrongs of the past.

We are often like little children standing there waiting

for our fathers to come to us and tell us they love us and they are sorry. Releasing our fathers in prayer, allows us to get on with our lives. It allows us to quit focusing on them in unhealthy ways.

Our unforgiveness of our fathers blinds us to any positive aspects of our fathers and could trap us into the same behavior. Abused children often become abusers. Children of substance abusers often fall into the same traps.

4.   The True Father

Luke 11:15-24 (NKJV) [15] *but some of them said, "He casts out demons by Beelzebub, the ruler of the demons."* [16] *Others, testing Him, sought from Him a sign from heaven.* [17] *But He, knowing their thoughts, said to them: "Every kingdom divided against it is brought to desolation, and a house divided against a house falls.* [18] *If Satan also is divided against himself, how will his kingdom stand? Because you say I cast out demons by Beelzebub.* [19] *And if I cast out demons by Beelzebub, by whom do your sons cast them out? Therefore they will be your judges.* [20] *But if I cast out demons with the finger of God, surely the kingdom of God has come upon you.* [21] *When a strong man, fully armed, guards his own palace, his goods are in peace.* [22] *But when one stronger than he comes upon him and overcomes him, he takes from him all his armor in which he trusted, and divides his spoils.* [23] *He who is not with me is against me, and he who does not gather with me scatters.* [24] *"When an unclean spirit goes out of a man, he goes through dry places, seeking rest; and finding none, he says, 'I will return to my house from which I came.'*

When the prodigal came to his senses he went home. In this parable, Jesus describes the love of His father. The father was going out every night looking for his son. The father loves his son and misses him. He has been praying for the time the son might come home. Then he sees him and runs to him. He did not wait with his arms folded for the son to come up and ask for forgiveness. Too many of us wait for the other person to beg forgiveness before we show our love for them.

The son said to him, "Father, I have sinned against heaven and against you. I am no longer worthy to be called your son."

The father went on to demonstrate his love. First the father gives him the best robe. The robe identifies him as a son. His old garments smelled of the pigsty. He gives the son a new, clean, garment to replace the rags he was wearing. When we fall in love with Jesus, the Father God gives us new robes of righteousness. When the Father looks at us, He no longer sees the garbage from the pigsty on us, He sees us the same way He sees Jesus. We can experience His love.

Then the prodigal's father puts a ring on his finger. The ring symbolizes authority. He gives the son all of his authority. The Father gives us His authority; He tells us. "You can do anything that I can do."

The prodigal's father puts sandals on his feet. Our sandals allow us to walk in the good works of the Father. Slaves went barefoot.

Then prodigal's father invites his son to his table. We are all invited to the Father's table. We often do not feel worthy to sit and eat at the Father's table. It all depends upon how much of the Father's love you can receive. See the Father loves you intimately. He likes us. His love flows to us but we often cannot receive that love because of our stuff.

We may never have had a father who was able to show love to us. The son returning from the far country did not feel lovable when he arrived at his father's house. But the father gave him the robe, the ring, and the sandals, so he would feel worthy.

Some Christians are able to walk up to the Father's table

and sit down. Others feel they have to sneak up to the table and beg. If I pray hard enough, if I live pure enough, if I do enough good deeds, then God will love me and give me a blessing. At the Father's table we receive the love of God the Father. At the Father's table, we receive our inheritance, our identity, our healing, and our spiritual gifts.

Our inheritance

> *Romans 8:17 (NKJV) and if children, then heirs-- heirs of God and joint heirs with Christ, if indeed we suffer with Him, that we may also be glorified together.*

Being an heir means we get something for nothing. Someone else earned it and paid for it.

> *James 2:5 (NKJV) Listen, my beloved brethren: Has God not chosen the poor of this world to be rich in faith and heirs of the kingdom which He promised to those who love Him?*

Our inheritance is the Kingdom of God. Everything that is in heaven, we can receive now. The Kingdom of God is laid out on the Father's table. When you know and experience the Father's love, you can aggressively seek the kingdom of God.

> *Luke 12:31-32 (NKJV) But seek the kingdom of God, and all these things shall be added to you. Do not fear, little flock, for it is your Father's good pleasure to give you the kingdom.*

The Father loves you and wants to give you the kingdom; the problem is we have to be in touch with the Father's love. The Father loves to give us the kingdom.

Many people keep striving to make God love them. They cannot believe that the Father loves them. Knowing the Father's love changes the way you appropriate that love. It changes the way you approach God the Father.

At the Father's table is your identity

When sons come back to the Father they shed their old image. The prodigal son's identity was that of a slave. When we drift away from the Father's love, the enemy is there to give us a different identity. He wants to re-identify you as a bad person. When I drift away from God's love the enemy tries to convince me that my real name is rejection. You may have had other names, but when we return to the Father's love, we receive a new identity.

> *1 Corinthians 6:9-11 (NKJV) Do you not know that the unrighteous will not inherit the kingdom of God? Do not be deceived. Neither fornicators, nor idolaters, nor adulterers, nor homosexuals, nor sodomites, nor thieves, nor covetous, nor drunkards, nor revilers, nor extortioners will inherit the kingdom of God. And such were some of you. But you were washed, but you were sanctified, but you were justified in the name of the Lord Jesus and by the Spirit of our God.*

In this scripture, the Corinthians old images were of evil people. But then God came in and transformed their lives. But they were washed, they were sanctified, they were justified in the name of the Lord Jesus Christ and by the Spirit of our God. We are washed, sanctified, and justified. He has changed our names; no longer rejected, but accepted and loved. The enemy of our soul wants you to go back and be comfortable in that old name. But God has changed our identity.

He wants to identify you by whose you are. Abram's

name was changed from " God is exalted father," to Abraham, "father of multitudes." Peter was a fisherman - He became a fisher of men. The Lord has a new identity for each of us. As you come to the Lord's Table, He gives you a new name.

Our new name comes as we become intimate with the Father. In the mobilized church, everyone has a new name and is filled by the Holy Spirit and is secure in God's love and understands their own role.

At the Father's table there is Healing

Healing is the children's bread. On the table set before us is the children's bread. The Father's love is often the catalyst that brings healing.

Healing is not a theological issue it is a relational issue. When we know the Father loves us, it changes our whole perspective when we come to the Father's table for healing.

Often the problem or pain is rooted in an area which separates us from the Father's love. That is where the enemy builds his stronghold. Demons flee when the Father's love flushes through us.

The key to healing has often been the realization of the Father's love. Healing comes in our ability to receive the Father's love.

At the Father's Table we receive Spiritual gifts.

Proper perception of the Father's love enhances receiving the Spiritual Gifts. When we hear His voice better, that is a Spiritual Gift. If we have to work to receive the

Spiritual gift, it is a block to receiving the gifts.

Our ability to receive spiritual gifts depends on our ability to understand the Love of the Father. This is the intimate relationship with the Father.

The Other Brother

One of the saddest characters in the Bible is the other brother in Luke 15:25-32. This parable was directed to the Pharisees who complained that Jesus welcomed sinners to His table. The Pharisees worked hard to earn the love of God through good works. Religious striving leads to a resentful attitude. Religious striving is attempting to earn the love of God through good works. We all try to do this. Why? We try to earn a right standing before God by our own effort. We do not understand or experience His unconditional love.

Insecurities drive us to try to perform for God. This is what happened to the older son. The harder he worked the further out in the field he got. The further he got from the Father's love, the harder he worked. The harder he worked, the further away he got. That was the case of the Pharisees. In their attempt to faithfully observe the law, they drifted into self righteousness and turned away from an intimate relationship with their Lord. The farther they drifted away from God, the more their hidden insecurities drove them to follow increasingly stricter rules, still trying to earn God's love.

A sudden flash of resentment toward those around us may indicate we are somewhat like the older brother. A critical spirit toward others is another indicator. Coming in from the fields is difficult because it requires God's help. The older son does not come home easily; in fact, he is still outside when the parable closes.

One of the most amazing moments in the story occurs when the father leaves the party, goes out to the older brother, and invites him to come to the party. When we drift away from the Father's house, God's love compels Him to come and invite us back.

The elder brother could not see the sin in his arrogance, resentment, and condemnation of his father and his brother. Drunkenness and prostitution are easier to see and turn from than self -righteousness. But our Father does not give up on us. Jesus was the messenger from the Father inviting the religious brothers to respond to love and come home.

Repentance and Forgiveness

Asking for and giving forgiveness are both required. We often have to forgive others for things they have done to us. We find our forgiveness through the blood of Jesus.

Activity

- First, we acknowledge the faulty image we have of "Father."

We have strong denial mechanisms. Recognizing that our father failed us makes us come face to face with the imperfections of his love. Allowing ourselves to feel unloved by our fathers is an experience we will usually avoid at all costs.

- Next, we identify the specific faulty lenses.

Identification reveals the areas where our natural father failed to reveal God's true nature.

- Removal of faulty images requires us to forgive.

We come to our heavenly Father and forgive our earthly fathers in Jesus' name.

As we forgive our earthly fathers, our heavenly Father reaches down and takes the distorted glasses from our eyes so we can see Him clearly. He touches the pain of our childhood and heals our wounded-ness.

Forgiving our father should not be confused with blaming our father.

We cannot hold our father responsible for every difficulty we have experienced. We are responsible for our reactions to the problems. We made bad choices in our attempt to find love and happiness in our lives. Children are to honor their fathers and mothers.

We maintain a posture of respect and love while we work through these issues with God. To deal with these issues we have to leave behind our bitterness and estrangement and move towards reconciliation with our fathers.

Forgiving our father frees us from bitterness and releases us in other ways, too.

We no longer have to wait for our fathers to come to us and right the wrongs of the past. We are often like little children standing there waiting for our fathers to come to us and tell us they love us and they are sorry.

Releasing our fathers in prayer allows us to get on with our lives. It allows us to quit focusing on them in unhealthy ways. Unforgiveness can connect us to the same sins they did to us and at the same time cause us to overlook any of their positive aspects.

5. Motivation

There is a reason why some people are successful, while others with the same capabilities and same history spend their lives well short of their dreams and visions. The answer is motivation. Motivation is the set of reasons that determine your behavior. Motivation is what makes you keep going when things are tough. There are two distinct forms of motivation: Extrinsic & Intrinsic Motivation

Extrinsic motivation comes from outside of the performer. Money is the most obvious example, but coercion and threat of punishment are also common extrinsic motivations.

In sports, the crowd may cheer the performer on, and this motivates him or her to do well. Trophies are also extrinsic incentives. Competition is often extrinsic because it encourages the performer to win and beat others, not to enjoy the intrinsic rewards of the activity. Research has indicated that extrinsic rewards can lead to over-justification and a subsequent reduction in intrinsic motivation. Extrinsic incentives can sometimes weaken the motivation as well.

Intrinsic motivation occurs when people engage in an activity, such as a hobby, without obvious external incentives. This form of motivation has been studied by social and educational psychologists since the early 1970s. Research has found that it is usually associated with high educational achievement and enjoyment by students. In *Drive: The Surprising Truth about What Motivates Us,* author

Daniel Pink[14] describes how traditional forms of motivation may, in some cases, decrease performance. Pink cites studies conducted with college students in the USA and with villagers in central India. The results were consistent despite the obvious cultural differences.

The researchers found that as long as the task required only mechanical or routine performance, extrinsic rewards worked well. Higher pay given for higher performance yielded better performance. Reward and punishment motivated the people when they were required to just follow the rules. However, when the task became more complicated and required even a bit of conceptual or creative thinking, extrinsic rewards failed to motivate and even reduced levels of performance. Higher pay for solving puzzles, for creative thinking and for more complicated tasks had a negative effect on performance. Traditional (extrinsic) methods work well with small children, but as the children grow up these methods become counterproductive. Other studies cited by Pink identified three major intrinsic factors which have the power to motivate individuals engaged in other than routine tasks: autonomy, mastery, and purpose.

People are likely to be intrinsically motivated if they attribute their personal growth to internal factors that they can control, they believe they can be effective in reaching desired goals, and they are interested in mastering a task. This explains the "Starving Artist" or the writer that continues to write despite having no sales of his books.

---

[14] Pink, Daniel H. (2009-12-24). *Drive: The Surprising Truth About What Motivates Us* Riverhead Books Penguin Group

Abraham Maslow's [15] theory accurately describes many realities of personal experiences. Many people find they can understand Maslow as they recognize some features of their own experience or behavior which is true and identifiable but which they have never put into words. Maslow believes that humans strive for an upper level of capabilities. Humans seek the frontiers of creativity, the highest reaches of consciousness and wisdom. This has been labeled as a "fully functioning person", "healthy personality", or as Maslow calls this level, "self-actualizing person."

Maslow has set up a hierarchy of five levels of basic needs. Beyond these needs, higher levels of needs exist. These include needs for understanding, esthetic appreciation and purely spiritual needs. In the levels of the five basic needs, the person does not feel the second need until the demands of the first have been satisfied nor does he feel the third until the second has been satisfied, and so on. Maslow's basic needs are as follows:

1) Physiological Needs: These are biological needs. They consist of needs for oxygen, food, water, and a relatively constant body temperature. They are the strongest needs because if a person were deprived of all needs, the physiological ones would come first in the person's search for satisfaction.

2) Safety Needs: When all physiological needs are satisfied and are no longer controlling thoughts and

---

[15] Maslow, A.H. (1943). "A theory of human motivation." *Psychological Review, 50* (4), 370–96.

behaviors, the need for security can become active. Adults have little awareness of their security needs except in times of emergency or periods of disorganization in the social structure (such as widespread rioting). Children often display the signs of insecurity and the need to be safe.

3) Needs of Love, Affection, and Belonging: When the needs for safety and for physiological well-being are satisfied, the next class of needs for love, affection, and belonging can emerge. Maslow states that people seek to overcome feelings of loneliness and alienation. This involves both giving and receiving love, affection and the sense of belonging.

4) Needs for Esteem: When the first three classes of needs are satisfied, the needs for esteem can become dominant. These involve needs for both self-esteem and for the esteem a person gets from others. Humans have a need for a stable, firmly based, high level of self-respect, and respect from others. When these needs are satisfied, the person feels self-confident and valuable as a person in the world. When these needs are frustrated, the person feels inferior, weak, helpless, and worthless.

5) Needs for Self-Actualization: When all of the foregoing needs are satisfied, then and only then are the needs for self-actualization activated. Maslow describes self-actualization as a person's need to be and do that which the person was "born to do."

"A musician must make music, an artist must paint, and a poet must write."

These needs make themselves felt in signs of restlessness. The person feels on edge, tense, lacking something, in short, restless. If a person is hungry, unsafe, not loved or accepted, or lacking self-esteem, it is very easy to know what the person is restless about.

As Christians we have been "Born Again" be a part of what God is doing in the world today. We have a spiritual need to be about our Father's business. We have a spiritual need to cooperate with God in what He has planned for our destiny.

Man was created in the very image of God, Genesis 1:27. As tripartite beings we have a body, soul, and spirit. Our body consists of flesh, blood, and organs; our soul consists of our mind, will, and emotions, while our spirit consists of wisdom, conscience, and communion. It is this latter item which provides us our motivation to become all that God has called us to be, to know and realize the purpose for which He created us.

Our fleshly needs require that our physiological and safety needs be satisfied. Our soul requires that our needs for love, belonging, self-esteem, and self-actualization be satisfied.

But we will never be complete until our spirit is satisfied. Our spirit consists of communion with God, wisdom, and conscience. Our spirit can never be satisfied until it is in relationship with its Creator who created us in His image. The only way that our spirit can be satisfied is for us to be in a communal relationship with God. Out of this relationship will flow creativity, refreshment, and fulfillment. When our spirit is filled with the Spirit of the Lord there is no end to our ability to accomplish great things.

This relationship goes well beyond the fact that Jesus died on the cross for our sins so that we can have a relationship with God, the Father. Jesus distinguished between justification and sanctification, though not using those words directly.

Jesus told His disciples:

> *John 14:21 (NKJV) "He who has My commandments and keeps them, it is he who loves Me. And he who loves Me will be loved by My Father, and I will love him and manifest Myself to him."*

In the upper room before going to Gethsemane Jesus prayed:[16]

> *"I do not pray for these alone, but also for those who will believe in Me through their word; that they all may be one, as You, Father, are in Me, and I in You; that they also may be one in Us, that the world may believe that You sent Me. And the glory which You gave Me I have given them, that they may be one just as We are one: I in them, and You in Me; that they may be made perfect in one, and that the world may know that You have sent Me, and have loved them as You have loved Me."*

The only way our deep spiritual need for that intimate relationship with the Father can be realized is for us to have and keep Jesus' commandments. The most obvious

---

[16] John 17:20-23 (NKJV)

commandment Jesus gave us was to love one another as He has loved us,[17]

Another commandment:[18]

> *Go therefore and make disciples of all the nations, baptizing them in the name of the Father and of the Son and of the Holy Spirit, teaching them to observe all things that I have commanded you; and lo, I am with you always, even to the end of the age.*

Also, [19]And He said to them:

> *Go into all the world and preach the gospel to every creature. He who believes and is baptized will be saved; but he who does not believe will be condemned. And these signs will follow those who believe: In My name they will cast out demons; they will speak with new tongues; they will take up serpents; and if they drink anything deadly, it will by no means hurt them; they will lay hands on the sick, and they will recover.*

And[20]

> *And being assembled together with them, He commanded them not to depart from Jerusalem, but to wait for the Promise of the Father, "which," He said, "you have heard from Me; for John truly baptized with water, but you shall be baptized with the Holy Spirit not many days from now." ....."But you shall receive power when the Holy Spirit has come upon you; and you shall*

---

[17] John 13:34
[18] Matthew28:19-20
[19] Mark 16:15-18
[20] Acts 1:4-5, 8

be witnesses to Me in Jerusalem, and in all Judea and Samaria, and to the end of the earth.

So how do we satisfy our spiritual needs? We can start by loving one another as Jesus loves us. When we love one another we can be at peace with others.

Lack of peace will not only destroy our relationship with the Lord, but it will affect our physical and emotional well being. Wherever there is anger and bitterness, we are not able to drink from the well of the Holy Spirit. We become shriveled up and decayed. Where there is life and peace there is communion with God and creativity blossoms. We receive clearer revelation and are not fearful of what people might say or do.

It is impossible to love others when you are holding on to unforgiveness and bitterness towards anyone. Jesus tells us that we can only be forgiven in the way that we forgive others. Chapter 13 will help you to forgive others.

Another commandment we are to obey is to go and disciple all people groups, baptize them and teach them everything Jesus has taught us.

6.   The role of the Holy Spirit

It is often tempting to refer to the Holy Spirit as some ethereal force or power. Both the Hebrew and the Greek terms used for the Holy Spirit refer to breath or wind. So at times it is difficult to realize that the Holy Spirit is a person and is God. As a result we often mistakenly refer to the Spirit as "it" instead of "He." He is the third person of the Trinity: Father, Son and Holy Spirit. Any simplistic metaphor for the Trinity falls dreadfully short of describing God in three persons. While the word "Trinity is not used in scripture, God is referred to as Father, Son and Holy Spirit.[21] Our finite human language is too weak to accurately describe the metaphysical, let alone define the infinite God.

The Bible does use anthropological language in relation to the Trinity and particularly the Holy Spirit. It seems that the Holy Spirit has a personality. He teaches,[22] He tells us about Jesus,[23] He can be lied to,[24] He prays for us,[25] He has a mind,[26] He has a will,[27] He has feelings,[28] and He speaks.[29]

The Holy Spirit is pictured as gentle and tender as a dove.[30] R.T. Kendall expands on the dove metaphor and he

---

[21] Matthew 28:19; 2 Corinthians 13:14
[22] John 14:26
[23] John 15:26
[24] Acts 5:3
[25] Romans 8:26
[26] Romans 8:27
[27] 1 Corinthians 12:11
[28] Ephesians 4:30
[29] Revelation 2:7
[30] Luke 3:22

shares the story of a missionary couple, Sandy and Bernice, in Israel[31]. After they moved into their house near Jerusalem, they noticed a dove had moved into the eaves of the house. They believed that that was a sign from God confirming their mission. They began to notice a pattern in the dove's ritual, when there was a lot of noise in the house, such as slamming door or loud voices, the dove left. They did not want the dove to depart permanently so they decided to adjust their behavior. They saw a parallel between their dove and the heavenly dove, the Holy Spirit. It changed their lives.

The Holy Spirit is a person, with feelings, sensitivities, and a will. We need to be conscious of this and adjust our lives to maintain the presence of the Holy Spirit. This will then produce the fruit of the Spirit in us: love, joy, peace, longsuffering, kindness, goodness, faithfulness, gentleness, and self-control.[32]

The Holy Spirit Brings Life

It is the Spirit who gives life;[33]

A strange feeling came over me as we walked the streets of Bangalore, the capital of the Indian state of Karnataka. Earlier in Bombay and New Delhi, we had experienced the spiritual heaviness common to regions where Christianity is under attack.

This sense of dread slightly abated while passing through specific areas of the cities. Landing at Bangalore's Hal Airport, we noticed a less intense heaviness. It was as if

---

[31] Kendall, R.T. *Sensitivity of the Holy Spirit*
[32] Galatians 5:22-23
[33] John 6:63

some heavy weight had been removed. Bangalore is India's third most populous city with eight and a half million people and has become the high tech capital of India. While on a shopping trip to Brigade Road we passed beggars old and young beseeching us for money. Our guide informed us that for most of the beggars it was their business and they lived fairly well. The shops on Brigade were selling everything from hand crafted Indian pottery and hand woven rugs to the latest in electronic gadgetry. As we rounded a corner, the spiritual heaviness lifted and my spirit seemed to jump with joy. Nothing in sight accounted for the change. No Christian church, no figures, or pictures. Then as we looked up, there on the top of a four story building, was a large billboard advertising a Christian evangelistic crusade. The sign in big, bold letters, two feet high, read,

"Are you having problems with your children? Are you having problems with your spouse? Is your life a mess?

Come meet my Friend Jesus!"

The date on the billboard had recently passed, but that feeling inside me was the Holy Spirit witnessing to my spirit, that Jesus was here now in this predominately Hindu city. The Holy Spirit had been released to move on the people of Bangalore and freedom had come to many people who had been oppressed by the enemy. Life had come to Bangalore.

Where the Spirit of the Lord is, there is liberty.[34]

> *Romans 8:11 (NKJV) 11 But if the Spirit of Him who raised Jesus from the dead dwells in you, He who raised Christ from the dead will also give life to your mortal bodies through His Spirit who dwells in you.*

The Holy Spirit is our teacher:

> *He will teach you all things, and bring to your remembrance all things that I said to you.*[35]

The Holy Spirit speaks:

> *He will tell you things to come.*[36]

Prior to leaving for India, a person had prophesied to me that there was a divine appointment for me in India. That same day on the streets of Bangalore my spirit again jumped inside of me as an elderly woman approached. Her trappings and cross on a chain around her neck indicated she was a Christian minister of some kind. As we passed, no words were spoken, but there was powerful connection and an acknowledgement that Jesus was indeed our Lord.

The Holy Spirit empowers:

> *But you shall receive power when the Holy Spirit has come upon you;*[37]

The Holy Spirit emboldens:

> *They were all filled with the Holy Spirit, and they*

---

[34] 2 Corinthians 3:17
[35] John 14:26
[36] John 16:13
[37] Acts 1:8

spoke the word of God with boldness.[38]

The Holy Spirit provides transportation:

The Spirit of the Lord caught Philip away[39]

The Holy Spirit directs:

Acts 16:6-7 (NKJV) Now when they had gone through Phrygia and the region of Galatia, they were forbidden by the Holy Spirit to preach the word in Asia. After they had come to Mysia, they tried to go into Bithynia, but the Spirit did not permit them.

In moving toward your destiny and realizing your God given purpose, two groups of people will look askance at you and tell you that you are doing it all wrong. The first group will explain that it is all to be done by taking a battery of tests to determine what you are best suited for, then you are to select a career that is on the growth cycle. You cannot be too careful. Make sure you have a job. The opposing group will quote scriptures which direct you to move in the Spirit and do not plan anything, just follow the Spirit. The correct path is to use a balanced approach: making plans, listening and being obedient to the Lord's direction.

Proverbs 16:9 (NKJV) A man's heart plans his way, but the LORD directs his steps.

Proverbs 16:1 (NKJV) The preparations of the heart belong to man, but the answer of the tongue is from the LORD.

---

[38] Acts 4:31
[39] Acts 8:39

Proverbs 24:3-4 (NKJV) Through wisdom a house is built, and by understanding it is established; By knowledge the rooms are filled with all precious and pleasant riches.

Proverbs 24:3-4 (MSG) It takes wisdom to build a house, and understanding to set it on a firm foundation; It takes knowledge to furnish its rooms with fine furniture and beautiful draperies.

Activity

Describe how have you felt the Holy Spirit leading your steps?

7. Values

The subject of core values has become a popular topic in business and organizational literature because a system of values will determine what we do and how we will act and react in situations. Much about who we are revolves around the things that are most valuable to us. Value is a concept that describes the beliefs of an individual or culture. Values are considered subjective and vary across people and cultures and may include ethical/moral values, doctrinal/ideological values, social values, and aesthetic values.

Personal values are related to choice. They guide decisions by allowing for an individual's choices to be compared to each choice's associated values. Personal values are developed early in life and may be resistant to change. They usually are derived from particular groups or systems, such as culture, religion, and political party. However, personal values are not universal; one's genes, family, nation, and historical environment help determine one's personal values. Each individual possess a unique conception of them i.e. a personal knowledge of the appropriate values for their own genes, feelings, and experience.

Groups, societies, or cultures have values that are largely shared by their members. Members take part in a culture even if each member's personal values do not entirely agree with some of the normative values sanctioned in the culture. This reflects an individual's ability to synthesize and extract aspects valuable to that individual from the multiple subcultures to which they belong.

If a group member expresses a value that is in serious conflict with the group's norms the group's authority may carry out various ways of encouraging conformity or stigmatizing the non-conforming behavior of its members. For example, imprisonment can result from conflict with social norms that have been established as law.

Core values are important because they become the base upon which your life, career, or ministry stands. The late John Wimber, who was responsible for the growth of the Vineyard movement, likened the building of a church to the constructing of a building. Before the foundation was laid there was the excavation.

> *Values are unseen but influential. Values are like the excavation within which the foundation of a superstructure is placed. Values set the location and the limits of activities. They are there but out of view. You do not think about values but they affect what you think, and as a result, what you do.* [40][*John Wimber*]

Activity

To help your determine your core values, we have prepared a list of typical values. Read the list and check those that are important to you. Go though the list again and this time, circle any and all of the values that you would cross the bridge for.

---

[40] Wimber, John "Building a Church From the Bottom Up" Church Planting Seminar, February, 1993, Anaheim Vineyard

Add any values that are important to you but not listed.

Acceptance	Accountable	Action-Oriented
Ambitious	Approachable	Attractiveness
Authority	Balance	Biblical
Boldness	Challenging	Caring
Cohesion	Commitment	Compassion
Competence	Confidence	Confrontational
Consistent	Contentment	Conviction
Cooperation	Creativity	Credibility
Curious	Cutting Edge	Decisive
Dedication	Depend on God	Determined
Diligence	Discipleship	Distinguished
Edifying	Efficient	Effective
Empowerment	Encouragement	Enthusiastic
Entrepreneurial	Equality	Example
Excellence	Evangelistic	Family-Oriented

Faithful	Friendship	Fruitfulness
Fulfillment	Generous	Goal Oriented
Godly	Stewardship	Gracious
Growth	Happy	Healing
Healthy	Helpful	High Energy
Honesty	Hope	Humility
Imagination	Innovation	Integrity
Issue-oriented	Joyful	Kindness
Leadership	Love	Power of God
Maturity	Mercy	Nurture
Obedience	Open	Orderly
Organized	Passion	Patience
Peace	People-oriented	Persistence
Positive	Proactive	Problem solving
Progressive	Purity	Reconciliation
Relationships	Relevant	Reliability
Reputation	Respectability	Responsiveness

Rewarding	Righteous	Serious
Safe	Service	Spirit Led
Teamwork	Thorough	Trustworthy
Unselfish	Unity	Visionary

Go back through the items you have circled and narrow it down to only five. If all you had left in your life were five values, what would they be?

Now, rank them in order, one through five.

Then for each value, write a definition, a statement of what it means to you to be successful in that area. If you put "family," what does a good family man or woman look like to you? If you put "spirituality," how will you know you have succeeded at being a spiritual person?

8.   Gifting

Jane [not her real name] was a gentle lady, serving in the church quietly, not asking for recognition. You hardly even knew she was around; until she discovered her purpose in life. At the board meetings she hardly ever spoke, but when she did it was with a passion. Jane had a passion for refugee families and could not understand why others did not have the same passion. She and the small group she led accomplished miracles, bringing refugees from war torn Viet Nam, Cambodia, and Ethiopia and then housing them and helping them to assimilate into the American culture. Because of her passion, Jane she attracted several others to her cause. As the ministry grew she dreamed of the whole church getting involved and how that could change the refugee problem. However much of the church leadership was already involved heavily in other ministries and did not have time to take on the refugee issue. Jane took this rejection personal.

There were others in the church who felt called to new ministries, such as a healing service and local evangelism outreach to the neighborhood. Each of these competing ministries were taken as a threat to the growth of the refugee program Jane headed. She did not realize that everyone in the church did not have the gifts of mercy and hospitality that were required to take in refugees. Jane had a gifting and a call to reach refugees; she knew her call and was devoted to its accomplishment. Others had different gifts and different callings felt their time should be devoted to other ministry areas such as local outreach and ministering to families across the nearby border in Mexico. As of this writing Jane's ministry continues as do a variety of other ministries of that church.

Entire church movements can be taken over by the enthusiasm, tenacity, and influence of one leader who pushes a particular form of ministry; signs and wonder, prophecy, or intercessory prayer. But the followers of Jesus are not defined by practices or programs, but by their core values.

We all are called and equipped for that call. We all have God-given, natural talents such as music ability, athletic prowess, intellectual gifting, or other things at which we can excel. The saddest situation is when a person feels they have no gifts or talents. That is not true. God created each one of us for a specific purpose and He provided each one with the specific gifts and abilities to fulfill that purpose. The problem arises in our inability to identify the purpose for which we were created and identifying the gifts that we do have. When we identify the areas in which we are gifted, we then have a better handle on discovering our life purpose. This does not mean that we are able to do things without training and development of our abilities. A great athlete may have the talent to be a champion but if he does not train and develop his talent, he will never become a champion.

Have you ever wondered why certain things appeal to you? Why you feel some things are more important than others? Have you ever wondered why people are the way they are? Why they don't seem to understand things the way you do?

The Bible speaks specifically about spiritual gifts in several places, but we want to take a look at those listed in Romans 12:6-8. The gifts listed here are known as the "Motivational" gifts because the Lord has given everyone a combination of these gifts to motivate them to accomplish the purpose for which He created them.

Everyone has a unique combination of talents and gifts, given to us by the grace of God whether we are believers or nonbelievers. They enable us to live and enjoy life, and fulfill our purpose. They are gifts that motivate you to fulfill God's call.

> *Romans 12:6-8 (NKJV) Having then gifts differing according to the grace that is given to us, let us use them: if prophecy, let us prophesy in proportion to our faith; ⁷ or ministry, let us use it in our ministering; he who teaches, in teaching; ⁸he who exhorts, in exhortation; he who gives, with liberality; he who leads, with diligence; he who shows mercy, with cheerfulness.*

This passage identifies seven different motivational gifts; prophecy, ministry, teaching, exhortation, giving, leadership, and mercy. A new book[41], "Motivation, your guide to fitting in," contains a complete explanation of these gifts and includes a spiritual gifts questionnaire that will tell you which gifts you possess.

Prophecy

The original sense in Greek was "one who proclaims," although soon the idea of "one who predicts" also occurred.[42] The verb *prophesy* has the twofold sense "to proclaim" and "to be an oracle prophet." Prophecy denotes a. "ability to declare the divine will," b. "proclamation," and c. "prophetic office." Prophecy is declaring the heart throb of God to His Church for the

---

[41] William F. Johnson & Rita H. Johnson, Motivation, your guide to fitting in, Aslan Press, 2014 available through Amazon or http://www.aslanpress.com
[42] Theological Dictionary of the New Testament: Abridged in One Volume.

purpose of edification, exhortation, and comfort.[43] The gift of prophecy is not a skill, aptitude, or talent. It is the proclamation of messages received from the Holy Spirit.

There are certain members of the body who have a special gift for prophecy but all believers are called[44] and are expected to prophesy the word of the Lord as the Spirit leads. Those with the spiritual gift of prophecy tend to have a unique blend of personal characteristics that might identify them in a group.

1. They usually have an urge to express their thoughts verbally. They are verbal people and they often think aloud, while those without this gift would consider their words carefully before speaking.

2. People with the gift of prophecy usually have an ability to discern difficult situations and the motives people quickly. As a result, they make quick decisions and judgments. When a person with this gifting is out of balance and does not listen to God, they may be quick to correct people who are not their responsibility.

3. They tend to be impulsive in their actions. They usually are able to decide quickly between right and wrong and can be very persuasive when dialoguing with others. When they are acting in the flesh, rather than the spirit, they will jump to conclusions and make judgments too quickly when they do not have all the facts.

---

[43] 1 Corinthians 14:3
[44] 1 Corinthians 14:1

4. Persons with the gift of prophecy will tend to reject people who do wrong, so that justice is done and so that other people are warned. But they may also judge, expose and cut off a person rather than making an attempt to restore them.

5. They are honest and open about their personal faults and failures and willing to suffer for doing what is right.

6. When they lose sight of the Lord, they may lack cautiousness and tactfulness in expressing opinions. They often will give prophecy to the Body that was meant for them personally.

The Gift of Ministry/Serving/Helps

The word translated here for ministry actually means service. It is distinct from to serve as a slave, to serve willingly, to serve for wages, and to do public service.[45] The concrete sense is basically to wait at table, to care for, and to serve. It has the idea of self-sacrificial service. Service comes as a result of divine prompting and is the spiritually-sensitive recognition and response to a particular need within the community.

Those with the spiritual gift of ministry/serving/helps tend to have a unique blend of personal characteristics that might identify them in a group.

1. They care about things being done. These are the people

---

[45] Theological Dictionary of the New Testament: Abridged in One Volume.

who will set up the chairs for a meeting without being asked. They are the ones who are always making sure that everything is ready. They can look at a room or at a project and see what has to be accomplished. And, they will not rest until all is done. They have the ability to see practical needs before others are aware of it and then want to do something about it.

2. They have a joy in serving which, they feel, frees other people to do "more important things".

3. They have a special ability to remember likes and dislikes. They remember the kinds of flowers, food, and movies a person likes, and use that knowledge to serve the person.

4. They receive a special enjoyment in taking care of physical needs of other people. At times they may be too persistent in giving unrequested help.

5. Servers need appreciation that confirms that what they have done is necessary and satisfactory.

6. They work best when given clear instructions, but when not listening to the Holy Spirit they may ignore proper authorities to get the job done their way.

7. They work best on short-range projects and get distracted when working on long range projects and tend to get flustered when they are rushed because of time constraints.

8. They have a strong desire to be with people.

9. Servers often have a real hard time saying "No." As a result they will take on more work than they can handle and will wear themselves out physically and emotionally. They may neglect home responsibilities because they are so busy out doing things for others.

10. Servers tend not to delegate.

11. When they lose sight of serving God, they may be hurt when the one they help does not acknowledge their service.

The Gift of Teacher

This word denotes teaching and learning in the wide sense of imparting theoretical and practical knowledge with the highest possible development of the pupil as the goal.[46]

The Gift of Teaching is the supernatural ability to explain clearly the truth of the Word of God with the goal of bringing Christian maturity. While those with the gifts of prophecy and exhortation make good teachers, their methods and motives are significantly different from those with the gift of teaching. This will be seen when we describe the characteristics of each.

---

[46] Theological Dictionary of the New Testament: Abridged in One Volume.

Characteristics of those with the gift of Teaching

1. They enjoy researching and presenting all the facts. They have a special ability to notice details. They are concerned with the accuracy of the details in their teaching and as they learn from others. While they are concerned with the growth of the person they teach, they are most concerned with the correctness of the material.

2. Teachers have a tendency to be silent until they have heard all the information presented by a speaker and then judge it based upon its accuracy. They care about truth. They care about the correct and incorrect kind of truth.

3. Credentials are important to teachers. Often a teacher, who does not know his audience, will present his qualifications before beginning his talk. He will explain where he went to school, where he learned his subject, and who his mentors were.

4. Teachers like to know the credentials of someone before they will hear them. And, they will check out statements made to verify the truth. When they are not in balance they have a tendency to become proud of their own knowledge.

5. Normally, teachers will not tell you personal stories but will stick to data and facts.

6. There is a danger that they may become intrigued with what scripture calls "vain" philosophies: ideas and

systems that really do not go anywhere but sound really fascinating.

7. The teacher may at times put all his or her dependency in a system of knowledge instead of in God.

8. Teachers who are out of balance do not give proper value to the practical wisdom of uneducated people and tend to criticize sound teachings because of technical flaws.

9. They can bore listeners with details when they give information that lacks any kind of practical application and focus on research.

The Bible list many teachers; Aquila and Priscilla,[47] Timothy,[48] Thomas,[49] and Luke in his Gospel and the book of Acts.

Gift of Exhortation

Exhortation is the ability to console, exhort, and encourage people to grow and to meet life experiences successfully. This gift might be called "the gift of encouragement to personal progress."

Those with the spiritual gift of exhortation/encouragement tend to have a unique blend of personal characteristics that might identify them in a group.

---

[47] Acts 18:1-3, 24-28

[48] 1 and 2 Timothy

[49] John 20:24-28

1. Exhorters are able to discern someone's emotional and spiritual state and are able to speak to them in ways which they are able to accept. The encourager wants people to clearly hear and understand what they are saying. Exhorters want to explain things logically and they will often provide a plan described in detailed steps of action.

2. Exhorters usually want face to face interaction. They want to observe the person's body language to make sure that the person understands the encouragement and coaching they are providing.

3. They have the ability to identify with different types of people, especially those that want to grow. The Apostle Paul said, "I become all things to all people so that I might win some."[50]

4. They want people to come into full spiritual and emotional maturity and for them to develop mature, harmonious relationships with one another and with Jesus

5. Exhorters make good teachers. Their primary motivation is to see people grow. An exhorter who is also a Christian wants people to mature as disciples. As a result, Biblical and experiential truth is important to the exhorter.

6. Exhorters are practical people. They look for steps and

---

[50] 1 Corinthians 9:22

practical ways for people to grow.

7. Exhorters who are not led by the Holy Spirit may impose unreal expectations on the people they are trying to help and minimize the effort that it will require for the person to achieve their potential.

8. Exhorters make excellent coaches and are good at mentoring. However, they may have a tendency to psychologically counsel, rather than encourage, when they fail to be led by God.

9. When an exhorter is out of balance, they may begin to treat people as projects rather than individuals. They may descend upon and try to fix people who have not asked for help.

10. Exhorters are not hooked on programs, but may be hooked on goals.

11. As the person grows, some exhorters tend to want to hold on to them. They like to have them around.

12. When out of balance, the exhorter may need the person to become dependent on the exhorter instead of God.

13. They have a tendency to trust what they see with their eyes more than what they perceive with the spirit. They may look at outward changes and wrongly think there has been an inward change.

14. When they are out of balance, they focus on life-related teachings and ignore basic Biblical doctrines. They are so focused on worldly things, they leave out Biblical truth.

15. When not listening to God, they may give advice before hearing all the facts and discerning the problem. They may trust in their own ability and ignore God's counsel.

16. Exhorters often look at problems and say, "Oh, what a wonderful opportunity to grow" without letting the person find that out on their own. People need to discover that in their own timing.

Well known exhorters in the Bible. Barnabus[51], whose name means "Son of Encouragement," is the most obvious exhorter. Silas,[52] Titus,[53] and Aaron also come to mind as encouragers.

Aaron often encouraged Moses in Exodus, Leviticus, and Numbers.

The Exhorter motivates people to live the Word.

The Gift of Giving

The Gift of Giving is the spirit motivating individuals to take that which they have, and share it with others for their support, thus freeing them up to do the ministry to which God has called them. The Gift of Giving could well be called the Gift of Support. The "Giver" is motivated to give of his assets and resources to support others. Just like all the other

---

[51] Acts 4:36; 11:22-2
[52] Acts 15:22-40;   1 Peter 5:12
[53] 2 Cor. 2:13; 7:6; Gal. 2:1

gifts, all Christians are called to give, but some are given the Spirit inspired gift of giving beyond what others are called to give.

There are five categories of giving: sharing of material goods,[54] sharing of spiritual things,[55] sharing the Gospel, sharing one's life,[56] and sharing of finances from one's own assets.[57]

There are a set of unique characteristics possessed by those with the spiritual gift of giving. The gifting is often recognizable by these traits.

1. A Giver has keen discernment about financial investments and has the ability to make money and accumulate assets. This is a God-given ability.

2. A Giver has the ability to test people's faithfulness and wisdom in how they use the gifts and wants to be a part of the ministry that he supports.

3. A Giver is discerning about the ministries others may propose to him to support. He or she will want their giving to be used wisely.

4. A Giver usually does not make quick decisions about giving as he needs God's direction on the gifts. He is not motivated by human appeals and will give at the Lord's

---

[54] Luke 3:11
[55] Romans 1:11
[56] 1 Thessalonians 2:8
[57] Acts 4:36,37

prompting. He will seek the Lord before making decisions about giving.

5. A Giver may use his giving to motivate others to give to the same cause. They really care about supporting others in their ministry.

6. A Giver prefers to give quietly and wants to avoid publicity[58].

7. A Giver needs his actions to be confirmed by the church. Confirmation by the spouse is also important. The spouse should always be involved in the decision making process where finances are concerned.

8. Things are not important to a Giver and they are not concerned about their status.

9. It upsets a Giver to see others waste money because he is able to see how that money could be used for ministry.

10. A Giver not only gives of his financial resources but also of his time and talents.

11. When a Giver is out of balance, he may become too frugal with his own family. They themselves do not need much and they do not understand why other family members need more. They are also aware that money can corrupt, and do not want to corrupt the family. Again, spouses should confirm the decisions. It is really

---

[58] Matthew 6:3

important, if you are a Giver that your children are not deprived of too much because what they see happen is you giving love to everybody but them.

12. Givers who are not hearing the Spirit regarding giving are prone to listen to unscriptural counsel on money use and may put excessive pressure on others to give.

13. When Givers fail to discern and follow God's prompting on giving, they will jump too quickly in their decision making without checking with their spouse and God.

14. When they are not following God's direction, Givers may attempt to control people or ministries with their gifts. They do this by trying to make sure that gifts are used in a specific area or way. They also may become "cause" oriented rather than people oriented, and invest in projects which primarily build the institution rather than benefiting people's lives.

The Giver supports the Word.

The Gift of Leadership

The gift of leadership is the special ability that God gives to some members of the Body which enables them to understand clearly the immediate and long range goals of a particular unit of the body of Christ and to devise and execute effective plans for the accomplishment of those goals.

Those with the motivational gift of leadership have a

unique set of character traits that identify them as leaders.

1. The have the ability to visualize the final results of a major undertaking. They can see all the way to the end of a project and are able to take the final results and break the process into smaller, achievable tasks with specific goals.

2. The can see and understand what resources are required and available for the activity. They will see all those things even before anything begins.

3. They have a tendency to focus on the ultimate goal and pay less attention to the distracting details.

4. They have the ability to delegate and know what should and what should not be delegated.

5. Their joy comes in seeing the parts come together in a finished project.

6. They have the ability to motivate, inspire, and encourage workers by their cheerfulness, approval, praise, and challenges.

7. They are willing to receive negative reactions from both insiders and outsiders in order to reach the goal, but they also require loyalty and confidence from those who are being directed and served.

8. When out of balance, they begin to look at people as resources rather than as people with needs. They may be accused of using people for their own ends.

9. Related to that, Leaders may become oblivious to the needs of others and put too much on them until they begin to feel resentful and over-burdened.

10. They may lose sight of other's feelings and focus too much upon the project.

11. When they are not led by the Spirit they may fail to delegate and become over committed and over worked.

12. If the leader is out of balance he or she may show favoritism to those who seem most loyal and ignore that person's faults while overlooking any serious character faults in a valuable worker.

The Leader FACILITATES the Word.

The Gift of Mercy/Compassion

The gift of mercy is the special ability that God gives to certain members of the body of Christ to feel genuine empathy and compassion for individuals, both Christian and non-Christian, who suffer distressing physical, mental or emotional problems, and to translate that compassion into cheerfully done deeds that reflect Christ's love and alleviate the suffering.[59]

1. Those with the motivational gift of Mercy are generally

---

[59] Wimber, John, Spiritual Gifts Seminar, Vol. 1, Vineyard Ministries International, 1986

considered "loving" types. They are the "teddy bears."

2. The gift of mercy equips one to sense in others such emotions as joy, happiness, pain, and despair. They care most about how people feel, as a result, they may be susceptible to making decisions based on feeling instead of reason.

3. They are the ones who bring home the strays and befriend those who have no friends.

4. They want to remove spiritual turmoil from others and bring them healing comfort. Many nurses and counselors are mercy people. They seek out those who need help and develop a personal ministry to them.

5. While the gift of exhortation helps people with words of love, the gift of mercy helps people mainly through deeds of love. They usually do not have to be asked; they see the need and just do it.

6. Their first response to someone else's problem is to ease the pain. At times they may rescue a person too soon. This occurs when they fail to ask God, "Should this be fixed?"

7. They engage in one on one relationships. They make and require deep friendships with mutual commitment.

8. Kindness comes naturally to mercy people and they expect no repayment.

9. They tend to be attracted to those with the Gift of

Prophecy. That can be a problem because those with the Gift of Prophecy care most about truth, while those with the gift of mercy care about feelings.

10. Christians with the special gift of compassion often feel led into the special ministry of intercessory prayer.

11. At times, mercy people fail to be firm and decisive when it is necessary. They want to avoid hurting other people's feelings.

12. In empathizing with others, they are prone to take up offenses of those who have been hurt and reject anyone who hurts someone they care about. They may cut off fellowship from those who are insensitive to others' feelings.

13. Because they are emotionally sensitive, they are vulnerable themselves to deep pain and hurt.

The ONE with Mercy SENSITIZES the Word.

If someone in the body is ill, those members with different motivational gifts will respond in different ways. Gift of Prophecy will pray and intercede for healing, strength and endurance. The Teacher will probably take over some books, tapes etc. The Exhorter will be right there to encourage and uplift. The Server will take over meals, offer to clean the house, do errands etc. The Giver will take time to listen and share, take food and give them the container. The Leader will find out needs and organize the people to meet them. The Mercy person will want to know how they feel, hug them, weep with them, and stay right there until they are well.

The Prophet PROCLAIMS the Word.

The Teacher EXPLAINS the Word.

The Exhorter MOTIVATES to LIVE the Word.

The Server DEMONSTRATES the Word.

The Leader FACILITATES the Word.

The ONE with Mercy SENSITIZES the Word.

Activity

If you wish to identify your motivational gifts go to http://aslanpress.com to receive the free spiritual gifts book and inventory questionnaire.

Part 2 - Why am I here?

9. Where am I?

We were a small group, no more than eight people crowded into our living room seeking the Lord. We had moved two thousand miles from the Pacific Northwest to Ridgeland, Mississippi, to plant a new church. Upon our arrival we had joined with another pastor and had gotten that church established and growing. Now it was time for us to fulfill our vision for a new church in a different area of the Jackson metropolitan area. We had gathered a few people, mostly single young adults and had begun meeting in our home on Wednesday evenings. We started each meeting a period of intimate worship to the Lord using a boom box playing cassette tapes which Rita had carefully and prayerfully selected. Then there would be a teaching time, followed by prayer for anyone who had needs. Afterwards we would gather in the kitchen for fellowship and snacks.

One evening after Rita had pushed the "Play" button on the boom box, and we all had begun to worship, something unexpected occurred. We had been worshipping for a while and had begun to move into a more subdued and holy time when the mood was suddenly broken by what sounded to me like a riot going on outside in the street.

Trying to ignore the disturbance, I refocused my mind to the Lord and our worship but the noises got louder. Pushing the curtain back a couple of inches, I stared out into the evening dusk, seeing only the quiet peaceful street and a lone squirrel climbing the oak in our front yard. After closing the curtain and re-entering worship the noise ceased. Maybe I was just hearing things. Then it started over again.

This time it was louder and more intense. There were voices of people screaming and cursing as if there were a brawl in our front yard. Again, I turned and pushed the curtains back. Again, there was no one there and nothing amiss. Then the realization hit me. No one in our living room had heard what I was hearing. They were all continuing in their worship, oblivious to the noise and turmoil that I heard. The Lord was trying to get my attention and it worked.

"Okay, Lord, what are you trying to show me?"

Swiftly He took me to the top of a mountain overlooking a wide, barren, valley. The thought of this still puts chills in my heart. Across the valley were thousands of people marching up a shallow mountain to a crater at the top. It looked like an ancient dormant volcano that was coming back to life. Smoke and flames began to belch from the open crater, yet the people kept climbing the hill toward disaster. As they reached the top they realized that they were going to fall into the crater. They could not stop because the others coming up the hill were pushing them forward into the fire. As the Spirit took me in for closer look at the struggling people, He spoke again, "These people are perishing. You must warn them."

This incident was so real and so upsetting that I could not talk about it for several weeks, and whenever I did all I could do was weep. With those few words the Lord had given me my purpose in life[60].

We had to forego the teaching element of the meeting and spend the rest of our time praying for each other. This was nearly twenty years ago, but it is as real to me today as

it was then. Since that time - as a pastor, teacher, and writer, - it has been my purpose to warn people of the consequences of life without God, share the good news of the Kingdom of God, and give people hope in Christ.

Why were we created?

Why did God create us? Simply, we were created by God to have relationship with Him. He loves us and desires that we love Him and commune with Him as Adam and Eve did in the garden before the fall. The sin of Adam and Eve allowed sin to enter into paradise. God, who is absolutely holy, cannot fellowship with anything unholy which results in our separation from God. In His love for us, He made a way for our sins to be cleansed through His Son, Jesus Christ, who came into this world, lived a sinless life, and was crucified for our sins. It is not our righteousness that allows us this exalted state of relationship with God, but it is the righteousness of the Christ. Through Jesus, we can now fellowship with Him.

What are we to do?

As followers of Jesus, what are we to be doing here on Earth? The last words of Jesus before He ascended into

---

[60] Ezekiel 3:17

heaven are written in two places. In Acts chapter one, Jesus told His disciples

> *Acts 1:4-5 (NKJV)* [4] *And being assembled together with them, He commanded them not to depart from Jerusalem, but to wait for the Promise of the Father, "which," He said, "you have heard from Me;* [5] *for John truly baptized with water, but you shall be baptized with the Holy Spirit not many days from now*

> *Acts 1:8-9 (NKJV)* [8] *But you shall receive power when the Holy Spirit has come upon you; and you shall be witnesses to Me in Jerusalem, and in all Judea and Samaria, and to the end of the earth."* [9] *Now when He had spoken these things, while they watched, He was taken up, and a cloud received Him out of their sight.*

The last thing that Jesus told His disciples is the same thing He tells us: to wait until we are baptized with the Holy Spirit, and once we have received the power of the Holy Spirit we will be witnesses to Him in our neighborhoods, in our regions, and throughout the entire world.

In Mathew's Gospel, Jesus spells out what it means to be His witnesses.

> *Matthew 28:19-20 (NKJV) Go therefore and make disciples of all the nations, baptizing them in the name of the Father and of the Son and of the Holy Spirit,* [20] *teaching them to observe all things that I have commanded you; and lo, I am with you always, even to the end of the age.*

Jesus gives the church four imperatives: go, disciple, baptize, and teach. This statement seems very clear. So why has it been lost or distorted over the years. It seems that the church will do anything to avoid following Jesus' direction. Many mainline denominations spend most of their resources maintaining the institution rather than making disciples.

Many evangelicals spend their resources fighting cultural wars. Major denominations continue to lose membership while our culture continues to accept worldly values. The majority of young adults leave their parent's church and religious principles when they go away to college or out on their own.

The so-called "Great Commission" is the method Jesus passed along to His followers and by inference to the church today. Rather than hopelessly wring our hands as things seem to get worse for the church, we must be about the business for which we were commissioned.

While walking in his cornfield, novice farmer Ray Kinsella hears a voice that whispers, "If you build it, he will come;" then he has a vision of a baseball diamond. So begins the 1989 movie, "Field of Dreams," starring Kevin Costner. Kinsella's wife, Annie, is skeptical, but she allows him to plow under his corn to build the field. While the movie has great entertainment value, it is a fantasy. Unfortunately many churches have been sucked in by this fantasy - "If we build it they will come." In the past when denominational loyalty was prevalent and there were a limited number of choices, the "Field of Dreams" philosophy worked well.

Church in America has, for the most part, become a spectator sport - ardent fans watching their favorite teams from the bleacher seats, sitting in padded pews watching all the action down front. They stand up when there is an asterisk in the bulletin and sit down when there is none. They cheer on the pastor when he makes a point and squirm in their seats when he fails to score. God forgive the service that goes into overtime. This is their comfort zone. We are here in our church, with our own kind of people, fellow pilgrims plodding along life's journey. It is comfortable, but is it good? Is it God?

A few years ago, a pastor asked me to visit his church and help them figure out why they were not growing. He asked if I would give them some insight as to how they could become a more vital force in their community. Their city was several hours from my home so we spent the night at a motel.

The next morning I set my GPS to the address of the church building. After driving past the church twice without finding it, I had my first clue to their problem.

In our meeting, the staff and leadership explained how they had been a part of a fellowship in the next town but wanted to have their own church in their own city. They had been in existence for five years but had only added a few families to the original core group. They asked my opinion as to why they were not growing. The first item mentioned was their lack of visibility in the community. If someone was looking for a new church home, how would they know about their church? Then we talked about going outside of the church building into the community with some kind of outreach. Their reaction was stunning. They stated, "We believe in the sovereignty of God. He will send the people He wants to us." It was obvious they had the "field of dreams" attitude. Only one couple at the meeting agreed that they should do something to reach their community. The others expected that God would send them those whom He desired to be a part of the church. Their attitude was like that of a farmer who built a big barn and stood by the door and wondered why the hay did not bale itself up, come into the barn, and stack itself in neat piles.

This church's theological position against outreach was the major factor for stunting their numerical growth, but most churches in America have just as destructive an attitude toward going outside the walls of their stained glass aquarium. They may be too busy with their own priorities, they may want to go out but are not properly led, or they may just be afraid. So they stay in their comfort zone.

Go

Jesus' first imperative is that we are to go. We are called to step out of our comfortable church pew and move out into the streets and allow the power of the Holy Spirit to direct us to be witnesses of Christ.

Did you ever wonder why nothing much seems to happen in church? Has your church lost its excitement? The church was not created to be a holding tank for saints, waiting to meet "Up yonder in the sweet bye and bye." The church is called to a bigger purpose than keeping us comfortable. We are called to get out of our stained glass aquarium to share God's love with the world. Jesus commissioned the church to go!

"Where do I go?" you might ask. It really does not matter that much. Wherever you go, the Holy Spirit can set up witnessing opportunities. In his book *Mere Christianity*, C. S. Lewis comments that a boat cannot be steered if it is not moving, but once it is moving through the sea, a tiny rudder can steer a huge ship. As long as we are moving, the Holy Spirit can steer us to where we need to be.

Disciple

Jesus' second imperative in Matthew 28:19-20 is, "to disciple all peoples. Most translations read, "...make disciples of all nations."

There has been some confusion about the term "make disciples." The word "disciple" can be a verb or a noun. In the original Greek "disciple" is used as a verb. Jesus commissioned the church to disciple all peoples. The root of the word disciple implies two people entering into a relationship where a novice is helped along by someone with more knowledge and experience.

One who disciples another is likened to a catalyst in a chemical reaction. In chemistry a catalyst is a substance that causes a chemical reaction to happen more quickly, but is not affected itself. In modern business theory, a catalyst is someone making changes or facilitates change in others.

When a novice pursues the art of pottery, he searches for an expert potter willing to help him get started in the business. When both agree, a mutual relationship is established. If one wishes to pursue any career field three things are required: knowledge, wisdom, and skill. Knowledge can be gained through study, but wisdom and skill can only be acquired by interacting with a person successful in the field. One achieves his goal faster and more effectively by finding someone good at what is desired and becoming their disciple.

While we lived in the Seattle area, my then eight year old grandson visited. In his home town it rarely snowed and there were no mountains. He was finally going to get his chance to ski. With our rented skis, boots and poles we made our way out of the chalet onto the snow. It was overcast and windy, but a good day for skiing. After helping him on with his skis, I began to instruct him how to move around on his skis.

He did not want any help. He had watched people on TV ski and did not need help. As we headed for the bunny slope rope tow, we looked back, and there was my grandson floundering like a fish out of water. He fell and struggled mightily getting up. He took a step and fell over his skis. It was good that Grandma was in the lodge drinking hot chocolate; she would have rescued him. We waited patiently but did not offer any more help. Soon his pride was overcome by his desire to ski and he asked for help. Then we were able to disciple him in the art of snow skiing.

We cannot force our views on others, but we can be available when they need help. We can only be available if we go outside the church. In today's world most people with real needs are not coming to the church for help; they are turning to other sources.

Our task is to be like Jesus. When He walked along the shore and called out to prospective disciples, "Follow Me," Peter, James, and John did not hesitate. Jesus never allowed the beliefs of society to influence His position on issues. As the Apostle Paul said to the Corinthians, we must be able to say to people "Imitate me as I imitate Christ." Others will be attracted to us if we can be a hero, be real, and put others ahead of ourselves.

Baptize them

After we have begun to disciple someone, there comes a point at which a decision must be made - a decision to follow Jesus. Each person must make this decision. Baptism is often considered to be a rite of passage. The person being baptized makes a public testimony to his/her life changing decision to follow Jesus Christ and become a child of God with all of the rights and privileges.

But that is not all. The church, the body of Christ, welcomes that person into the family of God and makes them feel accepted. Baptism is, as are all elements of the Great Commission, about relationships – relationship with Christ and relationship with other believers.

After moving to a new city several years ago, my wife and I began to look for a church. At first we settled on a fellowship within a few blocks of our house. They were open and accepting and made us feel at home. We jumped in and became active. But later we realized there were theological issues which separated us from the leadership. While shopping in a Christian bookstore, Rita was sharing with the clerk our desire to find a new church. The clerk quickly suggested one a couple of miles away. Not wanting to make

the same mistake we had at first, Rita met with the pastor of the recommended church and discussed our concerns. Based on this we made the decision to make a change. It took several months as I had to divest myself of the responsibilities in the church near our house.

We began to attend the new church and felt welcomed, but there was something missing. The worship services were outstanding, the Biblical teaching was sound, the people were friendly, the pastoral staff was nurturing, and we were growing spiritually, but we never felt that sense of belonging. We went through the new members' class and joined the church, but we still felt like outsiders. As a year went by we saw others come, stay for a while, join the church and then we never saw them again. We were growing so we stayed while other new people left. This problem has been identified repeatedly throughout most churches and denominations. Many churches are unable to accept newcomers.

As you disciple people, make sure you can enfold them into a fellowship which will accept them, nurture them, and equip them to go, disciple, baptize and teach.

Teach

The fourth element of the Great Commission is to "Teach all I have commanded you." If you study the commands of Jesus closely you will find that His commandments were about relationship with God and with one another.

You will not find Him teaching His followers doctrine and theology. We are told to "Know God." That means to not just know about God but to know God personally and intimately. Jesus commanded His disciples to Love, "Love God, Love your neighbor, and Love one another."

In my mid thirties, I called myself a Christian. I was a member of a church, I even taught an adult Sunday school class, but I did not "Know God." I knew about God. The scripture passage, "God is love..." didn't mean a lot to me because I really did not understand love. To me, love was a currency that I would spend to get something from someone. Little did I know God was wooing me to Himself with His love. *Mere Christianity* by C.S. Lewis contains a chapter on Christian love which began to awaken something deep inside me. It made sense in an intellectual way, but had yet to penetrate my heart.

One Sunday morning the sermon topic was love. I do not remember the message, but again, something within me was awakened. At the evening service, the subject was again on love. It was not the message that got to me. It was the topic.

The Holy Spirit was convicting me that I knew nothing about love and that I wanted to learn to truly love my family and others around me. As the altar was opened for prayer, I was the first one down front. Falling on my knees before God, I simply prayed, "Lord, teach me to love." Immediately the Lord spoke almost audibly and I heard these words. "First, you must love Jesus."

At first I was confused. Not growing up in church, I did believe in God, but was unsure about how Jesus fit in. It was then the words of C. S. Lewis came to mind, "If you want to love someone, start doing loving things for them, then you will begin to love them."

Still on my knees at the altar I prayed a prayer that I had never prayed before, "Jesus, I love you." It felt so good I repeated it again and again. Speaking that prayer for the third time, it seemed that something inside of me snapped

and released a flow of warm liquid love that poured all throughout my entire being from the top of my head down to the tips of my toes. It was God immersing me in His flowing love. It felt as if someone had poured warm oil on my head that ran down my entire body covering my arms, torso, legs, and my feet. John Wesley shared that his heart was strangely warmed as he prayed in Aldersgate Chapel. It was not just my heart, but my entire being strangely warmed by the love of God poured out on me. My life was changed forever.

Disciples need to be taught many things, but first they have to know God and His love for them. They must be taught how to share that love with others.

The church remains in the world today to be a witness for Jesus Christ. To be His witnesses means we are to go out of the church building into the streets and byways to disciple, enfold and teach all people.

This is a huge task for the church. But the church is made up of individuals with differing gifts and abilities. We are not all called to do everything. We have been called to be a part of what God is doing in the world today.

It is up to us to search out and find our particular part of the work of the church. There is a short video titled, "The

Harvest," which is a parable of fulfilling the "Great Commission." At the end, it asks a question, "What will be your role in bringing in the harvest?"

10. Called

I, therefore, the prisoner of the Lord, beseech you to walk worthy of the calling with which you were called, with all lowliness and gentleness, with longsuffering, bearing with one another in love, endeavoring to keep the unity of the Spirit in the bond of peace. There is one body and one Spirit, just as you were called in one hope of your calling; [Ephesians 4:1-4 (NKJV)]

It was early in the morning and having completed engineering business in India, I was returning to the airport in Mumbai, [Bombay]. We passed several trucks picking up the remains of the homeless who had passed away during the night on the streets of Bombay. Filled with compassion for the people of this nation, I asked the Lord, "Why is it that in the world's largest democracy, with every social program known to man, millions of people live in poverty, die in the streets, and reside in huts built with cow dung, tin and tarpaper?" Before the question was out of my mouth the Lord responded, "Because they do not know my Son Jesus; they have no hope." It was then panic seized my throat. We all fear God's call, "Is He calling me to be a missionary in some far off land?" With trepidation my next question was, "Do you want me to be a missionary to India?" The answer came much later than I had hoped, "No, you can serve Me best by sharing what you have seen with the people in America." To say the least, I was relieved. It takes a passion greater than fear to accomplish God's purpose for your life.

Scott Wesley Brown incorporated this fear in his song

"Don't Send Me to Africa"[61]

Please don't send me to Africa, I don't think I've got what it takes, I'm just a man, I'm not a Tarzan, Don't like lions, or rivers, or snakes, I'll serve you here in suburbia, In my comfortable middle class life, But please don't send me out in the bush, Where the natives are restless at night.

By 1984 things were going great for my career, my family, and our ministry in a local church, but our entire life was all about to change drastically. Five years earlier we had a stable job with a large company, we were living on the beautiful Mississippi Gulf Coast and were attending a comfortable church. A phone call from Washington, D.C. interrupted our comfortable life. The man on the other end of the line asked me to join his company, move to the West Coast, and start a new division of a three month old company headed by a man I did not know. We had been brought together by a person we both respected highly. After five years my vision of the earlier years had come to fruition. Our division had grown rapidly. Along with this growth, my responsibilities, authority, and compensation had increased. But there was something wrong. I was living my dream life and career, but God was about to change my life forever.

God created you for a purpose. He has a plan for your life. His purpose and His plan compose the ministry for which you were created. Now, today, God is calling you to fulfill that purpose and realize your destiny in Him.

Unfortunately, many of us go through our time here on earth just allowing life to happen; we often do not realize

---

[61]www.scottwesleybrown.com/index.php?option=com_maianmedia&view=album &album=7

that the Creator of the universe has a purpose for us to fulfill. As a result, we never reach the full potential for which we were destined. We work hard our whole life without the thrill of accomplishment and the satisfaction of knowing our life meant something.

"You were fearfully and wonderfully made and marvelous are His works"[62.] I remember to this day the paraphrase by Bill Gothard[63], "God does not make junk." We were all born with innate creative talents, assigned by our God, to be used for His purposes. As His children, created in His image, we have His creative spirit resident within our makeup. Each one of us who claims Jesus as Lord has been called into ministry on His behalf; some to vocational ministry, others to lay ministry, but we have all been called to continue Jesus' ministry throughout the world. Each one has been given a specific set of spiritual gifts, equipping us for the task to which we have been called. Each one has a specific job description and geographical places where our ministry will flourish.

> *Ephesians 1:16-19 (NKJV) (I) do not cease to give thanks for you, making mention of you in my prayers: that the God of our Lord Jesus Christ, the Father of glory, may give to you the spirit of wisdom and revelation in the knowledge of Him, the eyes of your understanding being enlightened; that you may know what is the hope of His calling, what are the riches of the glory of His inheritance in the saints, and what is the exceeding greatness of His power toward us who believe, according to the working of His*

---

[62] Psalm139:14
[63] Bill Gothard's Basic Youth Conflicts Seminars

mighty power.[64]

Scripture clearly demonstrates that all believers are called.[65] Most of us will not argue with this, but many will have serious nagging questions, "What is my specific calling? Why have I not yet seen it happen? What should I be doing until my calling is realized?"

Maybe you are reading this book because you have these questions, or maybe you just want to confirm what you already believe. Whatever the reason, we pray that the time spent here will put you on the road to realizing your God-given purpose.

It is important to understand that realizing God's destiny is a process. In this process, there are three distinct phases: the called phase, the training phase, and the commissioning phase. The Training Phase often begins before the call and continues until the end of our earthly life. This phase will be long and often trying. Some give up because they are not willing to accept the training. During the training phase we must always be hungry for God, His presence, His Word, and His wisdom. We must humble ourselves and become a servant to all. And we must be willing to learn new things, to be able to grow beyond our perceived ideas and theology.[66] The Commissioning Phase can be just as short as the call, but it is usually accompanied by a heavenly encounter.

The Called Stage is usually the quickest and easiest stage. Mine happened at a men's retreat in the Volcan Mountains east of San Diego, near the town of Julian. The

---

[64] Ephesians 1:16-19 (NKJV)

[65] 1 Corinthians 1:26-27; 2 Thessalonians 1:11

[66] 1 Corinthians 2:7-16

afternoon sun was bright and warm as I sat on a rough hewn log and meditated on the Gospel of John. I came to the passage in the last chapter where Jesus is talking to Peter.[67]

It was as if Jesus was speaking directly to me, "Bill, do you love Me?" ….. "Feed my sheep!" I knew immediately what this meant. He was calling me into full time Christian ministry. This first step, the calling, is usually brief, while training will last for the rest of our lives.

A look through scripture gives examples of how God called certain individuals.

Moses:

Moses spent forty years as a prince being trained by Pharaoh to eventually rule Egypt. Then one day he saw injustice toward the Jews and tried to solve it using his own strength and earthly wisdom. As a result he spent the next forty years on the back side of the Midian Desert. His training phase lasted eighty years. It consisted of learning organization and leadership skills in Pharaoh's palace and desert survival skills in Midian. Broken, humble, and teachable, God could now use him for His purposes. When the Lord appeared in a burning bush, Moses' attitude was humble and contrite. He did not feel capable of doing what God wanted. Moses was no longer able to rely on his abilities and his earthly wisdom, but God had a destiny for Moses.

Jonah:

---

[67] John 21:15-19

As a prophet, Jonah was one of the best. And he knew it. When God sent him to Nineveh, Jonah knew that his preaching would start a revival and cause the Ninevites to turn to God. If they did, God could use them to discipline Israel. Jonah thought he was smarter than God so he ran the other way.

God had to take Jonah through severe circumstances to get him to Nineveh. At the end of Jonah's book, we see the prophet still at odds with God. The way Jonah told the story, though, I am convinced he later repented and submitted himself to God's leadership. In the Sistine Chapel in Rome, Michelangelo painted all of the apostles and the prophets. Art critics today say that none has a more radiant countenance than that of Jonah.

Paul:

Paul was knocked off his horse and called by Jesus to be an apostle to the gentiles,[68] but the Council in Jerusalem told him, "Don't call us, we will call you!" They sent him home to Tarsus[69] on the back side of the desert for fourteen years.[70] During that time he encountered God, was translated into heaven, and was finally ready when the church called. It was then that Paul and Barnabus were commissioned to take the Gospel to the Gentile nations.

You:

God has called you and He has been preparing you since birth. While it may seem that nothing has been happening, He has been teaching, maturing, and cultivating you into the

---

[68] Acts 9:1-17
[69] Acts 9:30
[70] Galatians 2:1

person you need to be to fulfill that purpose.

11. Training

Training to fulfill your destiny requires a series of tests. These tests will prepare you for the future the Lord has prepared for you. In God's providence you never fail. He will allow you to take the test over and over again until you get it right.

Abraham's destiny was to become the father of many nations and the entire world would be blessed by his seed,[71] yet Abraham was a hundred years old without any children and Sarah his wife was well beyond menopause. Abraham could have totally given up, but he did not waiver through unbelief. He knew that it was God alone who controlled Sarah's womb.[72]

How do you respond when you feel that God has promised you something and it has not yet been realized? What do you do when you are expecting something from God and nothing seems to be happening? God's call in our lives is not something that we plan and organize. It appears as something God births in us.

In the birthing process, there is the conception stage, the gestation period, then the birth. This parallels the phases of "Call," "Training," and "Commissioning." Interestingly, there seems to be a correlation between length of the gestation period (training phase) and size of the baby (commissioned into your destiny).

---

[71] Genesis 12:1-3
[72] Romans 4:16-25

The gestation period for a field mouse is seven days and the baby vole is about the size of your pinky finger nail. The gestation period for the elephant is twenty two months. We

can therefore expect that if our training phase seems to be lasting too long, our purpose must surely be great. Many of us are pregnant with the purpose and promises of God, we may have wrinkles and stretch marks, but we walk around with Abraham's quizzical expression on our faces. God gave us a dream,[73] but when will we see it realized? Take heart, if you have been waiting a long time for the fulfillment of your promise from God, know that when it happens it is going to be very good.

During the training phase there will always be testing. God gives us an expectation of His grace in our lives, but, there are always times of waiting as He trains us to be hungry, humble, and teachable. What we receive from God is always incompletely understood (by us) and that is part of the testing. That is where faith comes in. We always have to take risks. We have to take steps of obedience. We have to start on the journey. Abraham did not know where he was going, but he knew Who he was going with. The Bible says "Step by step we will enter the land."[74] As we walk our dream out, we will continually be tested. The Bible says regarding Joseph that his dream tested him until it came about.[75] You will never fail God's tests. If you fall short, He will give you the opportunity to retake the test.

If you find yourself going through the same trials repeatedly, you may be retaking the test. We hope to eventually respond correctly. We will be tested by fear,

---

[73] Psalm 47:4
[74] Joshua 1:3
[75] Psalm 105:19

delay, difficulties, and injustice.

Tested by Fear

Fear is a discourager; it causes people to give up before trying. Two major fears have haunted me - fear of failure and fear of rejection. When encouraged by classmates to run for student offices, I refused. I did not want to become vulnerable to rejection. Losing would prove that I was not liked, that there was something wrong with me. This fear kept me from trying. Writing had always been a fulfilling hobby, but I wanted to make it more than a hobby. Fear of rejection for years kept me from submitting items to publishers. On many occasions, I was asked to write articles for trade journals and papers for symposia because of my position and technical knowledge. That was not a problem since they came to me; I did not have to fear being rejected.

At writer's conferences, I met with book editors who liked my book outlines and requested manuscripts, but I was unable to submit a manuscript because of my fear. My desire to be a writer was not as strong as my fear of rejection. Then in 1993, the Seattle Pacific Christian Writers Conference sent out a request for submissions for a writer's contest in conjunction with their annual conference.

My fear of rejection was being replaced by a realization of God's acceptance allowing me the freedom to dust off an old manuscript, edit it down to size, and submit it to be judged. After years of being tested and falling short, that mere action of submitting was a breakthrough. It was a good article.

At the banquet when they read the Honorable Mention, third, and second place winners I was bummed out, but not devastated. I thought my article was worth at least an honorable mention, but I was at peace. I tuned out, until someone jabbed me and said, "They just called your name."

Beyond my expectations, I had won first prize. Later that evening an editor asked to publish the article in a forthcoming issue of his publication. Several months went by and no check and no contact from the editor. Then it came, the dreaded rejection letter. The editor had moved on to another publisher and the magazine was now moving in a different direction. Rejection is inevitable, but it is not terminal. For the first time, I was able to celebrate rejection. The rejection did not say my work was bad or I was bad; I knew it was good. It had won first place. I finally passed the test. Suddenly I was free to submit the articles to other publishers. The prize winning article was submitted to a publication with a larger circulation where it was published exactly as it had originally been written.

A pastor friend became despondent. He was an associate at a large church and hoped to eventually become its leader when the octogenarian pastor retired. He had invested several years in that church and now realized that the senior pastor was planning to turn the church over to his son.

After he shared his heart and we prayed about the situation, I asked him a single question. "If failure was impossible, and money was no object, what would you do?" His immediate answer indicated he had been thinking about it for a long time, "I would start my own church." This had been his dream, a desire of his heart, but he had not let himself do anything about it because of fear.

He had been held back by the "what if's." It was obvious to me and anyone that knew him that God had planted that desire in his heart. A few months later a new church was launched in a rented meeting room. Today that church is having a dynamic impact on that community.

Being tested by fear teaches us faith. Faith is a gift of God, not just the sum total of our experience with God. We can impart the gift of faith to each other. Faith works through love.[76] We impart that faith as the same faith that Jesus has in the Father. That is far beyond our faith. We do not know we need faith until we face fear.

Tested by Delay

When I announced to my wife, Rita, that God had called me into full time ministry, she was not convinced. Several people we knew were leaving established careers and entering ministry. We suspected that some were called and others were just jumping on a band wagon. Rita thought I was in the latter category. Realizing that full time ministry was difficult enough with the backing of your spouse, I did not want to go ahead until she was in accord. So I did not talk about it anymore, but, I did complain to the Lord. I sensed Him saying, "Don't worry, when the time is right I will take care of her." Five years later we were together on a flight to teach at a conference in California. While reading a book on prayer, the Lord reminded Rita of a time in her life when she had the desire to be a pastor's wife. It was at that point we began the journey of following God's call.

While waiting for Rita's agreement, I had been preparing myself by teaching at conferences and retreats, studying church growth, and learning about my spiritual gifts. Some of us have a tendency to run ahead of God. We sense a call and want to make it happen now. God will often use the cautiousness of a spouse to hold us in check until His time is right.

---

[76] 1John 4:18

Delays are also used by God to test how faithful we are to His call. When He calls, we begin walking out our promise, but then we get stuck somewhere in time. Abraham was 100 years old; Sarah was well past menopause. He was forced to maintain that stubborn hope that she was going to have a baby. As the delays test us, we are prone to lose hope. Why haven't the promises come true? The enemy will tell us, "Of course you are barren, look at you." Do not lose hope, that you are too old or not worthy of receiving God's promises.

Paul was called be become a missionary to the Gentiles, but was sent to the back side of the desert for fourteen years[77]. Moses spent forty years in Midian before God met him in the burning bush. Do not lower your expectations. Your assignment is the same as Abraham's; sustain a stubborn hope. Sometimes we feel our vision is dead. We may have to give up on our vision that we have been dreaming about for years. We let it go. "Lord, its dead, but I still worship you, Lord." But God is the God of resurrection.[78]

Tested by Difficulties

On my way home from a church meeting I was suddenly struck by sick feeling.

It was not physical; it was emotional. The meeting had been about the church's youth group. A parent informed us that his son was on drugs and that many of the youth of the church were also using. Our son Kevin was a good kid and a

---

[77] Acts9:30
[78] Ecclesiastes 3:14

typical teenager fighting all of the issues of that age group.

What I suddenly realized was Kevin's rebellion and isolation were a result of drugs and not just the youthful struggles with school and social life. At that moment, I was ready to abandon God's call because of the enemy's attack against my family. Just as quick, I knew that this was what Satan wanted. His minions were attacking my family to prevent me from answering God's call.

As we move toward our destiny there will always be difficulties which will cause us to wonder whether or not to give up on God's call and go back to the world we were leaving. In the middle of difficulties, we will want to take short cuts. We will have to make ethical and moral decisions. This also is a test.

2 Timothy 1:8-10 (NKJV) Therefore do not be ashamed of the testimony of our Lord, nor of me His prisoner, but share with me in the sufferings for the gospel according to the power of God, who has saved us and called us with a holy calling, not according to our works, but according to His own purpose and grace which was given to us in Christ Jesus before time began, but has now been revealed by the appearing of our Savior Jesus Christ, who has abolished death and brought life and immortality to light through the gospel.

Tested by Injustice

Isaiah 30:18 Therefore the Lord will wait, that He may be gracious to you; and therefore He will be exalted, that He may have mercy on you, for the Lord is a God of justice. Blessed are all those who wait for Him.

Pagans do not have expectations of justice, but in the

family of God, we expect justice. You expect leadership and your friends to be like Christ, but, they are human and fallible. Injustice tests our gratitude and humility. We are far more apt to be hurt and bitter in the family of God because we have expectations of Christlikeness and we allow ourselves to become open and vulnerable. We will be tested by injustice until we respond correctly to injustice. The human tendency is to try to get even. If you watch football on TV, you will often note that a player may often get away with a cheap shot on an opponent. While the referee may miss the cheap shot, the player who takes revenge by returning the favor will often be penalized. My most embarrassing moment came while serving as a junior officer in the Army. After a rival had twice caused me injustice, I was fed up and retaliated. I was caught and suffered a severe reprimand.

Properly responding to injustice is the correct answer to this test. We are told to wait for God to correct the injustice, but waiting does not equal passivity. We are to keep knocking on the door of the Judge and He will answer.[79] In Acts 4:27-31, Peter asks for justice because of persecution. The disciples ask God to carry out justice and vindicate Jesus' holy name. Solomon asked God for an understanding heart that he might discern justice. Then, God blessed him with finances and wealth beyond measure.[80]

How do we ask God that we might receive justice and get God to act on our behalf? First, we must repent quickly when convicted of sin. Then, we must avoid actions that

---

[79] Matthew 18:7

[80] 1 Kings 3:9

would hinder God from blessing us. Always walk in unity,

for there He commands a blessing. For others, we must demand and carry out justice where it is lacking. Speak up for Jesus. Look after widows, orphans, and the poor. Heal the oppressed and stop any perversion of justice. Pray for the sick, cast out demons, and bring a light to those in darkness.

God not only reimburses a person for damages against them, but additionally demands payment for pain and injury. The Bible teaches in the Old Testament that if you catch a thief stealing from you, he must repay twice the value.[81] If the stolen goods are particularly valuable or needed, the thief must restore four times the cost.[82] Proverbs 6:31 says, "Yet when he [the thief] is found, he must restore sevenfold." God's system of justice is that the thief must pay back seven times for pain and injury. He issues a judgment for a suffering settlement, as well.

The greatest biblical example of injustice is Job. After all the losses of life, health, livestock, houses, family, and finances, God restored Job's losses double when he prayed for his friends.

The Lord blessed the latter days of Job more than his beginning. When you are tested by injustice, make sure you are just in your actions, ask the Lord to give you justice and wait. The result will be a restoration of all that the enemy has stolen, plus compensation for your pain and suffering.

---

[81] Exodus 22:4
[82] Exodus 22:1

12. Passing the test

In the last chapter we listed tests which we must pass before we are able to realize our God-given destiny. These tests are fear, delay, difficulties and injustice. The circumstances of the tests are not the important issue. The important issue is our reaction to them. The tests themselves are external, but our reaction is internal. We do not have a lot of control over of the external issues, but we can change how we react to them. That means we can change, which may open the door to realizing our destiny.

Overcoming Fear

The Delta DC9-31 was too low. On approach to Boston's Logan Airport, we had just overflown a garbage scow heading out to sea. From the starboard window seat on the emergency exit row, I watched hundreds of white gulls circling the smelly boat seeking a late dinner as the sun was setting in the west. If one of our two engines were to ingest a bird, we were all dead. To the north, several power and sail boats headed home to avoid the foggy blanket coming in from the sea. Airport runway lights were no longer visible from my position. The aircraft banked sharply making its final turn final to intersect runway two-seven. This was a regular trip for me, and this landing always felt unsafe, but today it was different. We were too low and heading for a water landing.

The plane was now only a few feet above the inky black surface. The plane suddenly veered to starboard then back to port. Was the pilot swerving to avoid something or was he just correcting for a wind shift? The runway must be just ahead. Maybe we will make it. Time began to slow down to a crawl.

Giving my seat belt an extra tug, I braced for impact. We hit something. Broken and bending metal screamed like fingernails on a blackboard. Paper cups and newspaper pages flew past as oxygen masks popped out of bins over heads. Momentum caused the plane to continue moving forward as the fuselage split open directly in front of me. Then everything stopped; it was quiet for several seconds. Then, as suddenly as it began the silence was broken. Passenger's screams mixed with the sirens and flashing lights of fire engines and ambulances. Miraculously, I was unhurt. Releasing my seat belt, I got up and walked past the rescue teams bursting through the huge hole in the fuselage. Outside, looking at the wrecked aircraft, I thought, "I had better take the train home." This is the way it always ends, taking the train home.

It was only a dream, a recurring dream, and the fourth in less than a year. The situation was always similar. Only the type of plane and the destination city changed from dream to dream. But, this time there was another difference. One week after this dream, Delta Flight 723 to Boston landed short of the runway in poor visibility striking a sea wall about 165 feet to the right of the runway centerline and about 3000 feet short. All six crew members and 83 passengers were killed. I had taken this flight to Boston once a month for the past year. After Delta 723 crashed, Amtrak became my transportation of choice to the Northeast corridor from my home in Northern Virginia. The odds of another crash at the same place are astronomical, but near misses call for reasonable caution. Irrational fear limits our ability to accomplish what God calls us to do and will keep us from reaching our destiny. My unreasonable fears include heights, bridges, rejection, and failure.

I once climbed the 897 steps to the top of the Washington monument and then missed the view of the

Mall because I was afraid to look out the window. As a child, before walking across a bridge, I waited until a large truck drove across. Seeing that the truck had made it safely across, I would quickly sprint across to the other side.

The root of most of our fears is an issue of control. We are afraid because we are not in control. As a licensed pilot, I flew the company's Cessna 182 on business trips around the Midwest, without any fear. Fear increased directly in proportion to my separation from the controls. Flying commercial was scary. When we are in control, we can be very brave. Think about it, "When was the last time you were afraid? What were the circumstances?" The intensity of fear is indirectly proportional to the feeling of being in control. The more you feel you are not in control of a situation, the more fear you feel.

Barak, son of Abinoam from Kedesh in Naphtali, is an excellent example which illustrates how we can overcome our fears. As a Prophetess, Deborah received revelation from God as to what the Lord was going to do. The Bible does not tell us whether God spoke to her in a dream, a vision, or some other means. The word she received from God[83] was a call for Barak to step into his destiny and realize the purpose

---

[83] Judges 4:1-7

for which he was created. Deborah tells Barak what God has said, but Barak is not too sure. He looks at his army, his capabilities, and the size of the enemy's forces and is afraid. He tells Deborah, "If you go with me, I will go; but if you don't go with me, I won't go."

Deborah responded, "Okay, I will go with you, but because of your fear, the honor will not be yours, for the Lord will hand Sisera over to a woman."

Barak did not get credit as the one to personally defeat Sisera, the commander of Jabin's army. But, Barak and all who went with him did show real courage and did trust God. They went out against Sisera and his army with essentially no weapons. They went against a technologically advanced army with 900 chariots of iron and fought on a plane where they were at a disadvantage. Nevertheless, Sisera and his army were utterly defeated.[84] God granted them a great victory against great odds. God caused great rains to overflow the banks of the River Kishon bringing a flash flood. The muddy conditions made the chariots of iron a hindrance, not a help, in the battle.

Control is the root of most of our fears; Barak would have had no problem with fear if his army was greater than Sisera's army. When Barak realized that God was going out, demonstrated by the presence of the prophet, Deborah, Barak and his men became brave. God has infinite resources available for your victory, even when you cannot see what they will be ahead of time. Deborah was an encourager building up the faith of Barak and his men. Her encouragement was that God, as King, will go out before His

---

[84] Judges 4:14-15

people into battle.

The Old Testament is full of types and shadows, examples of how God works with His people for all eternity. In this record of fear, encouragement, courage, and victory, we have a glimpse of what we can expect from our Lord.

Barak is a type of us. He is every man or woman called by God who does not believe that he or she has the ability to accomplish that call. Deborah is a type of the Holy Spirit.

The Holy Spirit communicates to us God's call on our life. The Holy Spirit instructs us, encourages us, and leads us as we attempt to follow God. Barak wanted to make sure that the Holy Spirit was with Him. We have to know that God is with us. If God is with us, then we do not take credit for our achievement. It is utterly amazing how much can be accomplished when we do not care who gets the credit. We just have to know that God is with us.

It has been several years since my last dream of being in an airplane crash. On the Thursday before Pentecost Sunday I was on a plane from San Diego to an afternoon meeting in Oakland. The plane had just reached cruising altitude and the seatbelt sign was turned off. The umpiring crew from Padre's game the night before were laughing it up and telling wild stories in the row behind me. As we were flying directly over LAX, the captain came on the PA.

"Uhhh, we have a situation here. I'm not sure how to say this. But, oh well, I'll tell you what I know." There was a long pause before he continued. "We are returning to San Diego. There was a suspicious person who placed a package on the plane, and then he got off. The authorities have not been able to find him." Another long pause was followed by the declaration, "They think he might have placed a bomb on the plane."

Along with everyone on the plane, I immediately had the fear that this was it; I would soon be dead. Then I realized that I was not in control, but God was. If this was my time to meet Him, I was ready. It was not that I knew He would take away the disaster, but that either way, it was okay. I was flooded with His peace. When we landed we were greeted by a phalanx of emergency vehicles and ushered to the farthest point of the airport. The armor clad

bomb squad came aboard went to the overhead compartment a few rows behind me and removed a package. They carefully placed it in an armored container and carried it off the plane.

Arriving later in Oakland, it was too late to make my meeting, so I just went to my hotel room, got down on my knees and prayed. My prayer was not just to thank Him for the safe trip, but for the transformation in my life that allowed me to trust Him in all circumstances.

In Acts Chapter 4, Peter and James had healed the lame man at the entrance to the temple. The religious leaders had them arrested because they were proclaiming that it was in Jesus' name that the man was healed. The Jewish rulers who instigated Jesus' crucifixion arrested the disciples and threatened them with all sorts of punishment if they did not stop speaking of Jesus. Peter and James returned to their people and explained what the Jewish leaders had said.[85] Then they began to pray. They did not pray for the Lord to

---

[85] Acts 4:23

protect them from the religious leaders or protect them from imprisonment. They prayed for the Lord to give them boldness to speak Jesus' words and heal the sick in Jesus' name.[86]

We all have times of fear. How do we handle our fears, rationally or irrationally? We can overcome all our fears by accepting the fact that we are not in control, trusting in the One who is in control, and accepting His call on our lives.

As we make Him our King, we relinquish control of our life. This sounds easy, but working it out in real life is very difficult.

God has charged each of us with a mission. Some are called to be great artists, some to be great writers, some to build churches, some to build ministries. But fear often seems to hold us back: fear of failure, fear of what others might think of us, and fear that the cost will be too high. As a result there are books not written, paintings not painted, churches not planted, and ministries not started all because of fear.

Passion will help us to overcome our fears; "perfect love casts out fear.[87]" Passion has to drive us harder than our fear holds us back. We have to have a passion that is greater than our fear. Passion gets us out of bed in the morning. What are you passionate about? What will it cost you[88] to follow Christ? We can choose to go back to bed and pull the covers up so we cannot hear God, or we can obey God and

---

[86] Acts 4:29-30
[87] 1 John 4:18
[88] Luke 4:18

move into our destiny. Barak is listed in the roll call of saints.[89] He overcame his fear, made sure God was with him, and thus reached his destiny. He counted the cost and chose to follow God. The only way we can overcome our fears is to trust God and make sure He is with us.

---

[89] Hebrews 11:32

13. Forgive others

Open dissension permeated an independent church on the eastern side of the Cascade Mountains in Washington State. Two factions with differing visions fought for control of the church's future. After failing to bring the sides together, the pastor resigned and left the church. The remaining leadership called in a mediator in an attempt to bring the sides together. After a several hours of often heated debate, the mediator called for a break in the discussions. In hopes of bringing together the leaders in common effort, the mediator suggested a time of prayer, worship, and sharing of the Lord's Supper. One leader quickly spoke up, "We don't do communion in this church." Later the story came out. This church had been birthed out of church split and the leaders had never forgiven the leaders of the church from which they had split. Since the previous church had served communion every Sunday, they vowed never to serve communion in their church.

The two sides never did come together. One group left while the other stayed and brought in a new pastor. The church lasted another year before it died completely. What had been birthed in conflict and lived without forgiveness died in conflict and never forgave. The death of ministries and churches is a sad and dreadful thing. People always get hurt. Some are never able to recover.

> Romans 12:19 (MSG) "Don't insist on getting even; that's not for you to do. "I'll do the judging," says God. "I'll take care of it."

Injustice when done to us or our loved ones leads to a desire for revenge. You see it in schools, the work place, on the athletic fields and in the church. But Jesus not only taught us to forgive, He demonstrated forgiveness when on the cross He said,

> *"Father, forgive them, for they do not know what they do."* [90]

Jesus taught His disciples and us to pray that the Father "forgive us our trespasses, as we forgive those who trespass against us."[91]

Then Jesus adds that if we fail to forgive others their trespasses, our trespasses will not be forgiven. This tells us two things: we need to be forgiven and our forgiveness from God is not automatic. It is conditional on forgiving others. Some Christians do not believe that they can sin after they have accepted Jesus Christ, but our obedience to God is never perfect in this life. We still have a propensity to sin.[92][93] We all sin at times. If we do not think we do, then we commit the sin of pride. This does not mean that when we sin we lose our salvation, but sin breaks our relationship with God. Our sin separates us from God.[94] Our sins hide God's face from us. When our sins separate us from God, He does not hear our prayers.

But when we confess our sins to God and ask for His forgiveness, He restores that relationship.[95]

If you cannot think of anything for which you need forgiveness, pray and ask God. Then listen, and He will let you know what you need to confess and ask forgiveness for.

---

[90] Luke 23:34
[91] Matthew 6:12
[92] Romans 3:23
[93] Galatians 5:19-21
[94] Isaiah 59:1-2
[95] 1John 1:9

As we humble ourselves before the Lord and repent of our sins, He changes us.[96] If you want Him to hear your prayers, confess your sins and receive forgiveness. Even if we confess our own sins, we are still at risk if we fail to forgive the sins of others. When we hold on to a grudge and refuse to forgive others, we are treading on dangerous ground. There are severe consequences in not forgiving.[97] There are physical effects, emotional effects, as well as spiritual effects. Anger and bitterness towards someone or something causes chemical reactions in our bodies which release enzymes which may result in disease and difficulties. According to the Mayo Clinic, "Forgiveness will lead to healthier relationships, greater spiritual and psychological well-being, less anxiety, stress and hostility, lower blood pressure, fewer symptoms of depression, and lower risk of alcohol and substance abuse." [98] Forgiving others restores our relationship with God.[99]

Making the decision to forgive does not let the other person off the hook for what they have done. There are consequences to their actions.

Forgiveness lets the forgiver get back to his or her life without being bound to the one that hurt them. But what if the issue is one that is so bad it is impossible to forgive?

Steven, as he lay dying after being stoned, asked God to

---

[96] James 4:8-10
[97] Matthew 18:32-35

[97]www.mayoclinic.com/health/forgiveness/MH0013 1, Nov 23, 2011 – Forgiveness and letting go can lead you down the path of healing and peace.

[99] Matthew 8:14-15; Mark 11:25

forgive his killers.[100] Jesus and Steven in the Bible were able to forgive, but is it possible for us living in modern times to have the same love that allows us to forgive grievous sins committed to us or our loved ones? Gunner Payne was the man most responsible for leading John Wimber to the Lord. In 1952, Payne's fifteen year old daughter was brutally murdered. The subsequent trial of her murderer caused national attention when it became a test case for capital punishment. Gunner was able to forgive his daughter's murderer.

We first met Thomasine Crowe with her husband, Bobby, on a mission trip to Costa Rica in 1994. It was later we heard her testimony of forgiveness. It shows what is possible when anger and bitterness are laid down. In 1987 Thomasine's 26 year old son was brutally murdered during a robbery by the son of a pastor. Thomasine's anger and bitterness toward the murderer ate at her day and night. It was then a couple in her Shreveport, Louisiana church shared with her the need to forgive her son's killer. Thomasine made the decision to forgive her son's murderer. Later she went to visit him in prison and told him she had forgiven him. They began to correspond and she visited him again. As a result of Thomasine's forgiveness, Ricky Blackmon was able to receive the forgiveness of Jesus Christ. His sins were forgiven, but there were still consequences to his crime. On August 5, 1999, with Thomasine in attendance, Ricky Blackmon was executed[101]. Thomasine became active in an organization ministering to crime victims and their families, teaching them the need to forgive.

---

[100] Acts 7:60

[101] Michael Graczyk, Associated Press, Laredo Morning Times, August 5, 1999, P4a

How do We Forgive?

The first step required in forgiving others is to admit that you are also a sinner. We get so caught up with what has been done to us that we ignore the fact that we are far from perfect. Jesus went to the cross to forgive the sins of the world, but before the cross there was the Garden of Gethsemane. It was there that Jesus fell on His knees before the Father, humbled Himself and said, "Not my will, but Your will be done."[102] He laid aside His desires and again opened Himself up to do the will of His Father. Jesus calls us into Gethsemane. Before we go to the cross and forgive others, we have to look at ourselves and see what might be our motivation. Gethsemane is the place where Jesus, in prayer, laid aside His righteousness and became all that we are. We have to lay aside our self-righteousness. It is no longer important who is right. As Jesus took on our sin, we need to say, "Lord, show me my sin, and identify me with the sin of all mankind." If we do not lose our self-righteousness and identify with mankind's sin, we will never be free.[103] We will just put on our martyr hat and say, "We forgave them." Then each time we forgive, we will feel more like a martyr. After a while we cry out, "I'm tired, I can't forgive anymore. I'm done, I won't forgive anymore." As a result, our forgiveness is never completed. We never got down off our exalted position. A good way to begin our prayer to forgive is, "Lord, take me to Gethsemane with You until all those lines of who is right and who is wrong are lost in the sense of common shame at the foot of the cross."

Our second step in forgiving someone's injustice to us is

---

[102] Luke 22:42
[103] Isaiah 6:5; Nehemiah 1:5-7

to receive Jesus' act of forgiveness. Forgiveness is impossible

in our human flesh. We may think we have forgiven and we may feel we have forgiven, but our feelings can fool us.[104] We cannot force our heart to change.[105] We have to realize we cannot forgive anyone at any time. Only Jesus can enter our human heart and change it. Sin and resentment separate us from the Father, but the blood of Jesus cleanses us from all sin. We have to be able to receive God's gift of forgiveness. Then forgiving others can be simple. When we come through Gethsemane we know that neither the one who hurt us nor ourselves truly deserve to be forgiven. But through Jesus Christ, we can forgive the one who caused us harm.

The third step is harder yet. More than forgiveness is required. We are commanded to bless those who hurt us.[106] That means we are to pray for all manner of good things to happen to them. "Bless them, rejoice with them, and mourn with them. If he is hungry, feed him; if he is thirsty, give him something to drink.[107] In doing this, you will heap burning coals on his head. " The idiom "to heap burning coals on one's head" has been the subject of much speculation since the next statement is: "Do not be overcome by evil, but overcome evil with good." Perhaps, this was tied to an Egyptian custom of putting live coals on one's head as a sign of repentance. But for me, there is a more satisfactory explanation.

It comes from the Middle Eastern practice of spreading the fire. In small villages where coal or wood was scarce, one person was designated as the fire tender.

---

[104] Jeremiah 17:9
[105] Jeremiah 13:23
[106] 1 Peter 3:9
[107] Romans 12:14-21

It was his responsibility to stay up all night keeping his fire burning. Early in the morning, he would take the coals from his fire, put them in a large pot, set the pot on his head, and go from house to house. At each hut he would take a hot ember from his pot and lay it in the fire pit igniting the prepared wood. The result of blessing the one who hurt you would be to turn him from an evil doer into the spreader of warmth in the community.

Activity

Take some time and ask the lord to show you anyone or anything you need to forgive.

- Family member

- Friend/enemy

- Church or ministry

- Pastor/former pastor

- Spiritual leader

14. Removing strongholds

2 Corinthians 10:3-6 For though we walk in the flesh, we do not war according to the flesh. For the weapons of our warfare are not carnal but mighty in God for pulling down strongholds, casting down arguments and every high thing that exalts itself against the knowledge of God, bringing every thought into captivity to the obedience of Christ, and being ready to punish all disobedience when your obedience is fulfilled.

Ancient fortified cities were generally built with a surrounding wall to protect the inhabitants of the city. These walls were strong enough to keep out invaders. The "wailing wall" in Jerusalem is a portion of the city wall that was destroyed when Titus attacked in 70 AD. The walls of Babylon were considered one of the Seven Wonders of the ancient world and were thirty meters thick at some points. During an attack, many soldiers stood on the walls to fight off attackers. If the walls were breached, the survivors would run into what is known as a "stronghold." The stronghold was a tower where fewer people were needed to defend. A stronghold is the hardest part of a fortress to break down. God is called our refuge, our strong tower. If we need safety, He is the One we run to.[108]

Strongholds, while designed for protection, may inadvertently cause us harm. They will protect us from what is outside, but we are held captive on the inside and not free to realize God's best. These are physical strongholds, but the Bible talks metaphorically about spiritual and soulish strongholds.[109] What the Bible calls strongholds, secular

---

[108] Psalm 18:2-3
[109] 2 Corinthians 10:2-6

psychology uses the term "Archetypes."

Strongholds are usually found in the mind, heart, or emotions of an individual. The person influenced by a stronghold does not understand how the Word of God is applied to particular areas of his/her life. They work through filtering and distortion by using wrong arguments, pretentions, or suppositions. As described in 2 Corinthians, a stronghold is speculation, thought, theory, or imagination that prohibits truth from being received. We construct these soulish strongholds to protect our deepest vulnerabilities, and they can keep us from achieving our God given destiny. Strongholds are not demonic by themselves, but the enemy can manipulate us through them by clouding our thinking. Strongholds are a powerful weapon against believers who are trying to realize their full potential and reach their destiny. They can be like puppet strings wielded by the enemy if the believer has not dealt with them through the cross of Christ. There is a war between light and darkness. If we have any darkness in us, the enemy will take every advantage against us and God's Kingdom.[110]

Strongholds can be cultural, spiritual, physical, emotional, or religious in nature: things you may have been taught i.e. racism, denominationalism. Strongholds lead us to wrong conclusions and cause us to resist the will of God. The person trusts in these falsehoods rather than relying on God. Strongholds affect our understanding of God, our doctrine, and our ability to recognize truth.

> *Proverbs 21:22 "A wise man scales the city of the mighty, and brings down the trusted stronghold."*

In addition to personal strongholds there are also

---

[110] 1 Peter 5:8; Romans 6:13, 13:12; 6:19; 7:5; 7:23; 1John1:6; Acts 26:18

"Corporate" strongholds. We call them traditions, beliefs, and philosophies.

In the 1930's in Germany, Adolph Hitler came into power. He promoted racism, the superiority of the Arian race, and prejudice toward the Jews. He stepped into a way of thinking which had been built up centuries earlier. Principalities and powers then moved that stronghold over the people blinding them from the light. Racial bias and hatred permeated the thinking of the culture. When this happened, people no longer were able to think clearly.

Newly married couples normally experience normal problems of adjustment as they learn to live closely together. As they learn to adjust and work through their issues, their marriage will succeed. But, when they begin to think about separation or divorce, a momentum seems to begin that cannot be stopped and reason is lost. They begin to spout the same line, "The kids would be better off." "She would be better off to find someone better for her." Their minds are helped by a stronghold wielded over them. The enemy will take you captive through your lusts, your sins, and your woundedness. He takes you captive to rob, kill, and destroy you.[111] We can see the result of personal and corporate strongholds influencing all of society today. In the political arena we see elected officials who no longer represent their constituents but have become opportunists, with one goal: power over others. In the economy, we see greed.

Even Christian business people exploit their customers and are as willing to cheat as non-Christians. The education community is intent on controlling the minds of young

---

[111] Ephesians 4:22-23

people. In sports and recreation, winning at any cost is the way to personal power. Even the church has done away with the Sabbath rest and encourages workaholics and the desire to be indispensable.

These are all the result of strongholds which are being wielded by principalities to keep God's people from their created purpose. The only way to break free from our strongholds is prayer. When a stronghold is wielded by a principality, it takes more than renewing the mind to win the battle. Spiritual warfare is involved. We need to remove the stronghold the enemy is using against us. First, it is necessary to bind the principality.[112] Next, the stronghold itself must be identified and dealt with. A pastor friend was constantly ill. Medical personnel could find nothing wrong. We began prayer ministry and met once a week for a month and nothing changed. One night, frustrated by the lack of progress, I challenged my friend icily, "Do you even want to get well?" After a long pause while he thought seriously about my question, he sheepishly replied, "I am really not sure. I feel so overwhelmed with responsibilities. If I were well, the people would expect more of me." His stronghold was that he was not capable of accomplishing God's purpose. Within a short time, the pastor was restored and has had a successful ministry of sharing the Gospel of God's Kingdom under the difficult conditions of ministry to the inner city.

Activity

What are the strongholds in your life that need to be torn down?

---

[112] Matthew 12:29

Part 3 - What do I do now?

15. Vision

Do you not say, 'There are still four months and then comes the harvest'? Behold, I say to you, lift up your eyes and look at the fields, for they are already white for harvest! [113]

At a pastor's meeting in California, we were reacquainted with a classmate from seminary who was planting a church in Colorado. Things had been going well for him, so we asked him to share his story. Two years before, we had left Washington State where we had helped plant a successful church, and moved to Mississippi with the intention of planting another church. With another leader, we had built a successful church, and then decided to plant one more in a different area of town. We had been into the new project for only a couple of months, but something seemed to be missing. My former classmate explained that the first thing he did upon arriving in town was to set aside two weeks of prayer and fasting in order to hear the Lord for direction. Sometimes in our busyness we attack a situation using our own ideas and our own strengths instead of

---

[113] John 4:35

seeking God's direction.

His plan excited me. As soon as we returned home to Mississippi, we began fourteen days of prayer and fasting. On the thirteenth day of the fast, just as we had settled into bed, the phone rang. It was a pastor we knew in Louisiana. He explained that he would be leaving his church to plant a church in a nearby city and was led to ask if we would be interested in taking over his church.

We had no desire to move. Rita had said she never wanted to move again. Besides, we were already planting a church in Mississippi. However, we had been praying and fasting for the Lord's direction. Maybe this was our answer. After telling him we would pray about moving, we hung up the phone, looked at each other and shook our heads. "No way will we move." We would call him in the morning.

We did pray about it and decided it could not hurt to go over and look. Then we were torn between what we were doing and what we could do in Louisiana. We contacted a friend and advisor and asked him to pray about the situation for us and let us know what he sensed. After a few days he called back and said, "I believe you have finished the work you were called to accomplish in Mississippi and are free to leave." He then gave me some very sage advice. He said, "Do not move until you have a vision for where you are going and what you will accomplish." A couple of weeks later while riding home from a meeting with a friend, the Lord showed me three goals which we were to accomplish through the new church in Louisiana.

To find out where you and your ministry are going, you must have vision. A Sunday school teacher once told her class, "When it is dark tonight, go into your back yard and count the stars." The next Sunday kids reported their counts:

one million, fifty thousand, five hundred, and then one kid proudly announced that he had counted twenty seven stars. "We have a very small back yard," he explained.

The Declaration of Independence that was passed by the Continental Congress on July 4, 1776, announced that the thirteen American colonies, then at war with Great Britain, regarded themselves as independent states and no longer a part of the British Empire. On that day in England, the King of England, King George, wrote in his diary," Nothing important happened today."

Our ability to see is not just with the eyes. Helen Keller was asked, "What could be worse than being blind?" She replied "Having sight, but not seeing." Vision is the ability to see beyond our limitations, beyond the size of our back yard.

According to John Maxwell[114,] vision requires four elements: (1) the ability to see, (2) the faith to believe, (3) the courage to do, (4) and the hope to endure.

The Ability To See,

The "ability to see" is our awareness of what is happening around us in both the physical world and in the spiritual world. King George was like the kid in the Sunday school class who had a small back yard. Many of us suffer from tunnel vision.

We are unable to see beyond our fences. If you truly want to realize God's destiny for you, you will have to work

---

[114] INJOY Life Club Volume 4, Lesson 10

hard to increase your awareness. We cannot limit the possibilities to what we can see in the visible world. We must learn how to listen to the Holy Spirit, seek the Lord, and spend time at His feet.

Many of us are so busy doing that we do not spend enough time being with Jesus. We are like Martha who needed to learn to be more like Mary.[115] We cannot limit ourselves to just the audible and the logical.

> *Psalm 121:1-2 I lift up my eyes to the hills, where does my help come from? My help comes from the Lord, the Maker of heaven and earth.*

The Faith To Believe

It was February 1991; "Operation Desert Storm" was about to end. We were leading a renewal event at a church a few miles outside the gates of Camp Pendleton, the home of the 1st Marine Division. The sun shone brightly nearly blinding us as my friend Mylon Nelson drove us to visit some shut-ins who could not make the meetings. Looking down at the handwritten directions in my hand it suddenly happened. Without warning, the note, my hand, and the inside of the car disappeared.

We had just turned onto Highway 78 and were heading west through the San Pasqual Valley. One minute, the bright sun bathed the countryside with brilliance, and then the next minute, I was blind. Fear and panic immediately set in, and then a strange peace came over me, and then, curiosity. There was this large a black hole in the middle of my vision.

Objects and light could be seen only around a thin

---

[115] Luke 10:41-42

periphery. Closing first one eye, then the other made no difference. The problem was with both eyes. Mylon strongly suggested we head for the nearest hospital, but at my insistence we continued to our planned destination with Mylon now doing his own navigation.

About twenty minutes later we arrived at our destination. Mylon led me up the sidewalk and rang the doorbell. We were greeted by an older gentleman and led down a dark hallway to the bedroom where his sister was lying in bed.

Somewhere between the doorway and the bedroom my sight returned as suddenly as it had left. It was then we realized that the man who greeted us was blind. He explained he had lost his sight as he was finishing a round of golf. It happened to him suddenly. One minute he could see normally; the next he was sightless. His description of what happened to him was identical to what I experienced with the exception that my sight had returned. We later considered the implications. Either the Lord had given me a word of knowledge of this man's affliction, or I had suffered the same affliction and the Lord chose to heal me. Theologically, it probably makes a difference, but to me, there was only one message: God is omnipotent; He is all powerful. In this life we are all vulnerable to sickness and injury. The only way we can live free of fear is to trust God completely. This incident gave me a new found faith which allowed me to step out in faith and follow the vision the Lord had given me to reach my destiny. I have to admit that that faith comes and goes at times, but I still trust Him completely.

Vision requires faith. Without faith, it is impossible to please God.[116]

We must believe that we can do all things through God Who strengthens us. Believing in yourself and in God requires faith. Can you see yourself writing a great novel, painting a vision from God, winning people for Christ? Do

you have faith to create great things, to accomplish great things? Jesus said, "According to your faith will it be done to you."[117] This is the "Faith Factor." Faith is a gift from God.

The Courage To Do

Faith requires action. It takes courage to be used by God. Joshua had the courage to step out in faith and to cross the Jordan River into the Promised Land. God gave Joshua the huge task of leading an entire nation into a hostile land and taking the land for God's people. There is a relationship between the size of the cause and the size of our courage. Courage rises when the cause is greater than our circumstances. The cause of gaining the Promised Land far exceeded the circumstances of wandering around in the desert for forty years. Courage falls when the circumstances are greater than the cause; therefore, our cause must be great. The cause we fight for is to rescue people from the grip of Satan and lead them into a relationship with Christ. There is no greater task. There is a cosmic war going on for the souls of humankind and we have been called to be soldiers in that war. Our flesh encourages us to live in our comfort zone; God encourages us to live in the courageous

---

[116] Hebrews 11:6

[117] Matt 9:29

zone.

Courage begins with fighting battles over our own character, self-discipline and will. Plato said the first and best victory is to conquer self. Pogo said, "We have found the enemy, and it is us." Our biggest obstacle is ourselves.

The Hope to Endure

Paul wrote:

> *"I have fought the good fight, I have finished the race, I have kept the faith."*[118]

To endure means to hold up under fire. To endure is to have the ability to withstand hardship, adversity, or stress; to remain firm under difficulty, without yielding. Winston Churchill wrote, "The nose of the bulldog is slanted backward so he can breathe without letting go." Cotton Mather, a famous Puritan pastor prayed for revival every day for twenty years. As he was on his death bed, the First Great Awakening began. So often we have the tendency to give up when the going is tough. We may think that God is closing doors and that we may be going in the wrong direction. It may be that the circumstances are bigger than our cause, but sometimes we just get tired and our faith begins to wane. However, this is the time to realize that the Lord may be testing us. Are we serious about following Him? Is He really leading us? James, the brother of Jesus tells us

> *Blessed is the man who perseveres under trial, because when he has stood the test, he will receive the crown of life that God has promised to those who love him.*[119]

Fresh Vision

A couple of dozen pastors, evangelists, and ministers of evangelical churches gathered for a small conference at a mountain park a few miles outside San Jose, Costa Rica. They had come to learn how to be more effective in making

---

[118] 2 Timothy 4:7
[119] James 1:12

disciples of Jesus Christ in their nation.

The North American leader of the conference had prepared several hours of teaching focused on revitalizing ministry and developing leaders. As the group slowly gathered, the speaker was led to throw away his agenda, notes, and expectations. The Costa Rican church leaders were coming as a last resort. They had been struggling for years in difficult ministries with little fruit to show for their efforts. They were completely exhausted and frustrated from ministries which had yielded little fruit. The conference leadership changed the agenda from a teaching meeting to a ministry time for the local pastors and leaders. First, there was a time of intimate and serious worship of the Lord, then a time of praying individually for each of the wounded attendees. The conference ended with a five minute message to the Costa Rican church leaders. The message was, "Get a fresh vision from God. If you don't have a fresh, clear vision of God's call, quit what you are doing and go sit at the Lord's feet until you receive that fresh vision."

As we realize our own limitations and see the needs around us, it is easy to become despondent. There is so much to do, and we are so weak, but we are only tools used by God to accomplish His purpose in the world and we serve a very big God. He is omnipotent. It is in our weakness that He is strong.

I can do all things through Christ who strengthens me. [120]

Seeing beyond our limitations creates enthusiasm, defines boundaries, produces effort, unites us, and rallies us. God will give you a vision of His purpose which will begin

---

[120] Philippians 4:13

to energize and excite you. Our tendency when seeking a vision of our future is to look at ourselves and our own capabilities. But if you want to find out what the Lord has in

store for you, do not look to yourself; look to God. If you have been struggling to find your God given purpose, you probably need a fresh vision from God.

Holy, holy, holy is the LORD Almighty; the whole earth is full of his glory.[121]

Before we can get a fresh vision from God, we will have to see our God in a new light. We need a fresh vision of God. Peter went fishing in the wrong place at the wrong time at Jesus' direction. As a result, he saw Jesus in a new light and was given a new vision.[122] Out in the Midian Desert, Moses was tending livestock when God called from a burning bush. He had a fresh vision of God and discovered his call.[123] Isaiah saw God and was forever changed.[124]

These men received a fresh vision of God, and then received their call and their destiny was realized. We all regularly need a fresh vision of God. This can only come as our relationship with the Lord grows deeper. If you want to receive a fresh vision from God, follow the pattern of Isaiah: Worship, Confess, Forgive, and Serve.

Isaiah was in the temple worshipping the Lord when he received a fresh vision of God. It was a vision of God's holiness.[125] John, the beloved apostle, received a new vision of God's holiness.[126] Holiness refers to God's nature.

---

[121] Isaiah 6:3b
[122] Luke 5
[123] Exodus 3:10-12
[124] Isaiah 6:1-9
[125] Isaiah 6:3b,c
[126] Revelation 4:8

Holiness means we have to believe that God is always right. We may not understand, but at the deepest part of our being, we know that He is right. We cannot judge God. In

this life we only see partly, but when we see Him face to face, we will understand.[127] We need to repent of judging God and realize His holiness. There has been a move in much of the church to place God on a human level, so that we might more easily understand His love. In the process we tend to lose the awesomeness and holiness of God. When the angels repeat, "Holy, Holy, Holy," it shows the completeness of His holiness. He alone is supremely holy.

> *"Woe to me!" I cried. "I am ruined! For I am a man of unclean lips and I live among a people of unclean lips,"* [Isaiah 6:5]

We need a vision of our own sinfulness. In the presence of God's holiness, Isaiah realizes his own sinfulness. This is a direct consequence of being in the presence of holiness. The closer we get to the holy God, the more obvious our lack of holiness becomes. We must be always be hungry for more of God and be humble before his awesomeness. We must become teachable: able to take correction. There is no room for ego or pride. It is not "what a great thing I am doing for God." We have to be in touch with our own sinfulness.

We need a vision of the condition of this world. Isaiah knew the sinfulness of the world in which he lived.

As we come closer to God and His holiness, we begin to understand the sinfulness of the world around us. At times we forget how far from God the world has gone. We look

---

[127] 1 Corinthians 13:12

around and begin to compare what is happening now with what has happened in the past several years and we think this is normal. Our normal is what God calls unclean. We have been like the proverbial frog in the kettle that is unaware of the water getting hotter and hotter. Suddenly,

when it is too late, the frog is cooked. In the presence of the almighty and holy God, we see what needs to be changed. Even though Isaiah knew that the world was loved by God, as we should, Isaiah also knew that the world was headed for disaster.

> *Then one of the seraphs flew to me with a live coal in his hand, which he had taken with tongs from the altar. With it he touched my mouth and said, "See, this has touched your lips; your guilt is taken away and your sin atoned for." [Isaiah 6:6-7]*

We need a fresh vision of the power of the word of God. As we look around at this sinful world, the task of bringing about change appears to be so great that it is impossible. Faced with an impossible situation, there are normally two possible actions for us to take.

"Type A" personalities will jump in and begin to do everything because there is so much to do. This does not work. Within a short time this individual will suffer burn out, possibly become ill, and lose his effectiveness.

Others will look at the situation, agree that it is impossible, and sit back and do nothing.

There is, however, a third option. This is the one which will accomplish the Lord's purpose and bring peace to the individual. Believe that the word of God has the power to save.[128]   Believe that the Lord has a role for you in His solution to the problems of the world. Find that purpose, and fulfill it. God will provide the purification[129] [130] for the world just as He does for Isaiah as we admit our sinfulness

and humble ourselves before Him. God has the power to transform the world.

"Here am I. Send me!" [Isaiah 6:11]

We need a fresh vision of our own potential. In spite of our sinfulness and weakness, we can do all things through Christ, who strengthens us. We have enormous potential when we are walking in God's calling. We do not get to define that call. We cannot just go do something and ask God to bless it. The call must come from God, and then we respond. We do not determine the size of our task; we say, "Here I am, send me."

Vision produces passion.

Activity

Behold, I say to you, lift up your eyes and look at the fields, for they are already white for harvest![131]

1. As you go through your day, take time to look around. Do not just look with physical eyes, but also, with your spiritual eyes. See the people around you.
2. Commit to a time of prayer and fasting.
3. Spend time in silence, listening to God.

---

[128] Romans 1:16
[129] Numbers 31:22-23
[130] Malachi 3:2
[131] John 4:35

4. Meditate on Scripture.

5. Ask God what He wants you to be doing in the future.

6. Keep a journal of what you hear in your quiet times.

16. Passion

"One person with passion is greater than ninety nine with an interest" [John Maxwell]

Who or what are you passionate about? Passion is the fuel that will keep you going through difficult times; it will motivate you to move out of your comfort zone and follow the Lord's leading. When God sees something that needs to be accomplished, He will often give a person a passion for making it happen. You often hear someone say, "Look at that situation, someone ought to do something." That means they have a passion.

In September of 1988, Chuck and Joan Hartzell shared their testimony during a renewal event at a church in the West Point Grey area of Vancouver, British Columbia. Friends had encouraged us to invite them because of the call on their lives and their passion for the poorest people in India. Years before we met, they had felt God calling them away from their comfortable lives in the Seattle suburb of Kirkland, Washington to something new, but as yet, they did not know what it would be.

Chuck was an orthopedic assistant with the Veterans Administration and Joan was a registered physical therapist and visiting nurse. After sharing this with their pastor at the Woodinville Community United Methodist Church, he introduced them to a missionary from India who was visiting at the church. The missionary shared stories and showed them pictures of the plight of the poverty, sickness, and hopelessness of the people in India. Soon, Chuck and Joan headed for India to help set up a medical clinic. They sold their house and gave away most of their possessions to live in the village of Kuppadi in Kerala state on the southwest tip of India. While helping with the clinic, they saw the plight of a caste of villagers who had been potters for generations.

Their ancient vocation was dying because of more efficient modern manufacturing processes. Aluminum and plastic pots had replaced clay pottery for cooking and cleaning. As a result, the pottery business was disappearing. So, too, were the hopes of these potters and their families. The Hartzells had an idea to start a small business where the potters could make their pottery while the Hartzells would sell the pottery in the United States. The Hartzells did not know how to make pots, but chose to learn so they could incorporate practices that would be acceptable for the U.S. market. Clay pots can no longer be used for cooking, but there is a market for clay decorative items in gardens and patios. When enough clay pots were completed, the Hartzells loaded a 20-foot shipping container and sent it by ship to Seattle and a distribution system was established in the United States.

As the people of Kuppadi began to trust them, Chuck and Joan began to teach them about Jesus and many came to know Jesus as Lord. God had given Chuck and Joan a passion for the people of India. They were used by God to bring the hope of Jesus into that corner of the world.

University of Colorado football Coach Bill McCartney had a passion for men in the church who were not being empowered. While in a room with seventy men, he caught a vision of stadiums full of men. The Promise Keepers ministry, which transformed the lives of millions of men, was born. Big dreams create a passion to bring about transformation.

Passion comes from vision. If there is no vision, then there will be no passion. If you do not see a need, you cannot be passionate about the need. Passion without vision is merely hype. John Wesley said, "I just set myself on fire and people come to watch me burn." John the Baptist said about Jesus, "He will baptize you with the Holy Spirit and with Fire!"[132] If you do not have passion, your vision is too dim. So many people lack passion because they have allowed something precious to become familiar. We want acceptance and approval so we try not to stand out or be unique. As a result, we settle for mediocrity, which is highly over-rated.

Passion leads us to strive for excellence. One of the major reasons for the declining of main line denominations is the lack of passion. Modernism, with its emphasis on reason, discouraged emotion in the church and in the Christian faith. Jesus commanded us to love God with our whole being.[133] Passion is defined as an intense, compelling emotion which is evidenced in decisive, courageous action.

When we lived on the Mississippi Gulf Coast we used to go crabbing. We would put an old chicken neck or wing in a wire pot and lower it into the water just under the pier. Then we would pull it up with several crabs fighting for the chicken. We put the crabs in a bucket. The bucket did not need a top because whenever one crab would try to crawl out, other crabs would grab him and pull him back down. That is the way with many folks in our world today. If anyone wants to escape the bucket of common life, others will quickly try to pull them back. This apathy tends to increase with age.

---

[132] Matthew 3:11
[133] Mark 12:30

Passion is the energy of our soul. According to John Maxwell[134] a passionate person is a goal oriented visionary, a self-starter, has an optimistic attitude, gives 100% all the time, strives for excellence, is creative about getting things done, accepts responsibility, doesn't make excuses or shifts the blame, believes in people, inspires others to do their best, and rises to leadership.

After vision, passion is the second step to realizing your destiny. If you are not passionate about anything, you need a fresh vision. Passion increases will power, changes lives, and will change you. At the heart of passion is intense desire: how badly you really want to accomplish something.

There is a story about a proud young man who came to Socrates asking for knowledge. He walked up to the muscular philosopher and said, "O great Socrates, I come to you for knowledge." Socrates recognized a pompous numbskull when he saw one. He led the young man through the streets, to the sea, and chest deep into water. Then he asked, "What do you want?" "Knowledge, O wise Socrates," said the young man with a smile. Socrates put his strong hands on the man's shoulders and pushed him under. Thirty seconds later Socrates let him up. "What do you want?" he asked again. "Knowledge," the young man sputtered, "O great and wise Socrates." Socrates crunched him under again.

Thirty seconds passed, thirty-five, forty. Socrates let him up. The man was gasping. "What do you want, young man?" Between heavy, heaving breaths the fellow wheezed, "Knowledge, O wise and wonderful..." Socrates jammed him under again. Forty seconds passed; then fifty.

---

[134] INJOY Life Club: Volume 9, Lesson 5

"What do you want?"

"Air!" the young man screeched. "I need air!"

"When you want knowledge as you have just wanted air, then you will have knowledge".[135]

When you have a passion, watch out for fire fighters. Fire fighters are those people that feel it is their responsibility to pour cold water on any fire they see in someone else. They focus on what is wrong with an idea rather than what is right. They have a questioning spirit; they hate change. Fire fighters keep many people with great potential from realizing their God-given destiny.

To keep your fires burning you need to stay away from firefighters, hang around fire lighters, attend fire lighting events, and attempt fire lighting deeds for God

Nehemiah

Babylon under Nebuchadnezzar had destroyed the Jewish temple in Jerusalem and carted all of the furnishings to Babylon where they stayed until the Medo-Persian Empire defeated Babylon. Cyrus, king of Persia proclaimed in 538 BC that the Jews could return to Jerusalem and rebuild their temple. [136] When Artaxerxes I became king of Persia in 445, the temple in Jerusalem was not completed and the situation in Jerusalem had deteriorated as enemies of the Jews kept them from restoring the city. The people were discouraged and had lost hope of living in peace. In December of 445 BC, a delegation returned from Jerusalem

---

[135] M. Littleton, Moody Monthly, June 1989, p 29
[136] Ezra 1

headed by Hanahi.

They told the Jews remaining in Persia of the deplorable situation in Jerusalem. Hanahi's brother, Nehemiah, worked as the king's bartender and was heartbroken over what he had heard. God gave him a burden for his people who were living in Jerusalem.[137] Nehemiah became passionate about the situation so he began to pray.

He mourned and fasted for days. He knew that God was all powerful and could change the situation with his people. When Nehemiah prayed he confessed his sins and the sins of the Jewish Nation. He placed himself and his people at the mercy of God and humbly pleaded for an end to the troubles. He accepted the call of God on his life and with the backing of Artaxerxes set off to lead the restoration of Jerusalem.

John Bright writes, "The reorganization of the community under Nehemiah saved the nation from disintegration and set it on the path which it followed for the remainder of the Biblical period."[138]

God will light a passion in whomever He chooses to accomplish His purpose. Just as He did for Nehemiah, God will give you a passion for a person, a group of people, or a situation. When you read the newspaper or see something on television is there a situation or are there people that cause you to weep or to wish that somebody would do something? That may be God stirring up a passion in you and calling you to fulfill your purpose.

When you feel yourself drawn to a situation that requires help, pray and ask the Lord to show you what your

---

[137] Nehemiah 1:4
[138] Bright, John; A History of Israel 3rd Edition, Westminster Press

role is to be.

Becoming Passionate

If you are not passionate about anything, then you will not realize your purpose in God. If we are not passionate, then we must become passionate people. Soren Kierkegaard is quoted as warning of the danger of the church losing its passion for the gospel and treating it instead like "a piece of information." Passion is replaced with descriptions of passion. The result for the church, he said, could be compared with reading a cookbook to a person who is hungry. God desires passionate followers.[139]

Weak desires bring weak results. Athens was about the only place Paul visited that he did not plant a church because he was greeted by a greater foe than open opposition – indifference.

If you lack passion, pray that God will give you passion, associate with passionate people and remember what God has done for you. We should always be passionate for God, our family, and our purpose.

Vision produces passion – passion produces discipline.

Activity -What is Your Passion?

1. When you watch the news on television, or read a paper, what brings tears to your eyes?

2. As you see people on the street, what kind of people do

---

[139] Titus 2:14; Romans 12:11

you hurt for?

17. Naming Your Future

Shirley (not her real name) was a lady that celebrated life. She was the type of person that lit up a room when she entered. She was quiet and unassuming, and her joy was contagious. Everyone felt better when she was around. In our worship service we always took time to allow people to express thanks to the Lord for what He had done in the past week. Shirley was always first to stand and express her praise for being able to be in church. You see, Shirley was dying of cancer, but she did not let her circumstances dictate her emotions.

She came into my office one day and shared a concern. Spending several days each month in the hospital undergoing cancer treatments, she noticed the concern and fears of patients and their families sitting around the waiting room.

"I feel that I am supposed to talk with them and pray with them," she explained, "But how do I go about it? Will the hospital be upset?"

Explaining that she did need permission from the hospital, I wrote a note to the hospital chaplain, a friend of mine, and told her to go see him and find out what she needed to do to obtain the hospital's permission.

The next day she came back beaming with the news. She had met with the chaplain and the hospital administrator. They had given her official recognition to pray with cancer patients and their families. But then she got a troubled look on her face.

"What do I do now? How should I proceed?"

My suggestion was to go into the waiting room and sit down, pray and ask the Lord who He wanted her to pray for, and then look around the room and that God would show her who to talk to and pray for. The next week she shared her experiences with the whole congregation.

For many months Shirley ministered to hundreds of patients and families - sharing Christ's love, forgiveness, and acceptance – until her sickness progressed and kept her away. When the cancer took her home to Jesus, she had fulfilled her destiny in the lives which were transformed and enriched by her ministry.

We each have the potential to do great things, but so far most have not lived up to our potential. Sadly, some never will. Most of us wander through life like a boat without a rudder. We allow life to happen to us and wonder why we have not fulfilled our destiny.

Bob Mumford[140] proposes three tests for discerning God's will: the word of God, the prompting of the Holy Spirit, and circumstances/opportunities. He likens these elements to range lights that ships utilize as they enter a channel or harbor. When the range lights are aligned, the ship captain knows he is on the right course to get the ship safely into the channel. I would add a fourth element in discerning your destiny: confirmation from a trusted friend or spiritual authority. What does scripture tell you about your calling? Where do you believe the Holy Spirit is leading you? Is there a door open for you to proceed? Have you shared it with trusted friends who have confirmed this call?

---

[140] Mumford, Bob, *Take Another Look at Guidance, Discerning the Will of God*, Lifechangers Publishing; 20th anniversary edition (June 1993)

When these all line up, you will want to write out a concise statement of your calling.

How many of you reading this book now can describe, in detail, what you desire for your future. Some may want to be rich, but do not know how to accomplish that. Some may respond, "I just want to be happy," but could not define what is meant by happiness. Many will respond, "I want my life to mean something."

In the chapter on Motivation, we discussed "Self Actualization" as a need that arises when basic needs have been fulfilled. In this chapter, we will provide a method for naming your future: defining what you really want to be when you grow up - your destiny.

Moses did not merely lead the children of Israel out of slavery in Egypt to escape the harshness and bitterness of life. They were not running <u>from</u> something, they were running <u>to</u> something.

Moses had a driving vision that propelled him to lead two million people through a wilderness of perils, obstacles, and interim defeats to a place they could actually see ("vision") in their mind's eye, "a land flowing with milk and honey."

This "Promised Land" was Moses' long-term vision. It was such a distinct, attractive, and compelling purpose that it drew his people, as if attracted by a powerful magnet, through enormous difficulties toward one all-attracting goal. Moses is a good study of the process of realizing destiny. He himself never reached the Promised Land. His destiny was to be God's agent, to codify what it meant to be God's people, and to lead the Jewish nation to its destiny: their land flowing with milk and honey.

Nehemiah wept when he heard about the plight of the people living in Jerusalem and realized he could transform their situation. His destiny was to restore the walls of Jerusalem in order to bring honor back to a helpless and hapless people.

When observing successful people, it is easy to see that, one way or the other, most have been driven by a very clear, compelling, personal sense of destiny. This usually began when they were able to see a need. Seeing the need stirred up within them a motivating passion to do something. Then, utilizing their values, gifts, and knowledge, they came up with an action plan.

If you have done the exercises in the previous chapters of this book, you probably have a good idea of your destiny. If not, you may want to go back and review those exercises.

Having a general idea of your destiny is not enough. The idea must be tangible and you must accept it for yourself.

In order for your vision and passion to empower you to utilize your values, gifts and understanding, there must be more definition. As you set about defining or naming your destiny, it might be helpful to picture the construction of a building. The building construction analogy has been used many times in building a ministry. Every building has a purpose: hospital, school, house, fire station, etc., yet all are similar in many ways. Each of us has a destiny which is unique to us because we have different gifts, callings and passions, yet we are similar in many ways.

When constructing a building, we think first about the foundation, but even before the foundation is poured, the land must be prepared for the foundation. The foundation will sit in an excavation. In building our ministry destiny, the excavation is represented by our values. Values are not visible to others, but they are very influential in everything we do. We have Biblical, cultural, and personal values. Our destiny is based upon our value system.

In our building construction analogy, the foundation and structural elements are represented by our priorities. Priorities give visual form to our values; they reflect our values. Priorities are based upon our passions. Priorities may be changed when our passions change while our values are difficult to change.

The infrastructure of the building – electrical wiring, plumbing, and air conditioning - are represented by our practices. Our practices hang on our priorities and could be likened to the actions that we take to accomplish our purpose.

Practices can be changed rather easily compared with our values and our priorities. Practices are the stuff that programs are made from and they are the principle reason

for growth or hindrances of growth. Programs are like the rooms of the building and are not permanent like values, priorities, and practices. Outsiders will only see the programs.

As you begin to name your destiny, look at the top five values which you identified in Chapter 7 and write them down here:

1. _____

2. _____

3. _____

4. _____

5. _____

From Chapter Eight, list below the three gifts that seem most appropriate to you. If you have completed the gift questionnaire[141] this will be much easier.

1. _____

2. _____

3. _____

List below those things that arouse your passion. Chapter 16.

_____

_____

_____

_____

If money was no object, and there was no possibility of failure, what would you do with the rest of your life?

_____

_____

---

[141] Bill & Rita Johnson, "Motivation, Guide to Fitting In", Aslan Press 2014, http://www.aslanpress.com

_____

_____

_____

Start with a single paragraph describing your destiny and what it will look like when it is fulfilled.

You will then want to weave in your values and priorities to form a succinct personal statement of purpose that crystallizes, in your own words and in your own way, your long-term goal.

When you lock in on such a statement, it generates a tremendous surge of momentum which keeps you on track in achieving your overall purpose in life. You will be in for a special experience of tapping into latent energy from within that can energize your entire being when you begin. The effect of doing so is like installing and activating a turbocharger inside your internal engine!

Your objective is to develop a statement of between 25 and 45 words-no longer. Avoid long, rambling statements. The more specific you can be the better. You might have three parts to your statement:

    a. A Foundational phrase:

        1)   "What do I stand for?"

        2)   "What is my foundation?"

        3)   "What are my core values?"

    b. An Action phrase:

        1)   "What do I want to do with my life?"

2)   "What do I want to be in my life?"

3)   "What am I building?"

c. A Results phrase:

1)   "What are the desired results of my life?"

2)   "What are the outcomes of my life?"

3)   "What do I want my life to leave behind when I'm gone?"

4)   "How do I want to be remembered?"

Remember, this statement is not set in concrete. You can revise it at any time. In fact, as you grow towards your destiny, new horizons will open up to you and you will probably find that your expectations of what God can do through you were limited by your beliefs about yourself.

Activity

In the next day or two, get in a quiet place and spend at least an hour working on your statement. It will probably take two or more settings to complete this, but it will be an important step in fulfilling your destiny.

18. Discipline

Discipline without passion can lead to legalism. Having a vision, a deep felt passion, and a statement of your destiny will not make it happen. The actions in your statement will require discipline to fulfill your destiny. In Matthew 13, Jesus taught about the kingdom of God using parables. In the parable of the "Pearl of Great Price" the merchant is seeking beautiful pearls. When he finds this one pearl, he sells everything he has to purchase that one pearl. That is discipline. How valuable is your vision? How passionate are you about your calling? What are you willing to forgo in order to obtain your destiny?

My wife Rita is a great oil painter. Her original art has been on display throughout the United States and some of her paintings are in private collections in places as far away as India and Korea, but she has not always been this great. The Lord put a desire in her heart to paint a vision she received when she was going through a very trying period in her life. Several years later she had the opportunity to take lessons. Her passion kept her persevering as she learned about color and painting techniques. She became focused on her painting and minor annoyances and illnesses did not keep her from her desire. Was this her pearl of great price? No, probably not, but she had a vision of what she could become, and a passion to paint one painting for her Lord.

Discipline has a lot to do with never giving up, but it also is about doing things right and doing right things. It is also about excellence. There are many individuals in the world that do just enough to get by and as a result, they never reach their destiny; they just exist and wonder why others pass them by.

In his book *100 Greatest Moments in Olympic History,* author Bud Greenspan writes

> *At the Olympics, glory doesn't only go to those who win. Dorando Pietri was in a state of collapse as he entered the stadium for the final yards of the 1908 marathon. The Italian fell five times before an official helped him cross the finish line. Pietri was disqualified, but his indomitable spirit made him an international celebrity.*

> *A similar display of courage enabled Derek Redmond of Great Britain to finish the 400 meters in '92. Hobbled by a torn hamstring near the half-way point, Redmond hopped the rest of the way with the help of his father, Jim, who rushed from the stands to aid his son.*

> *And who could forget the sight of Tanzania's John Stephen Akhwari, his right leg bloody and bandaged, staggering into the stadium more than an hour behind the winner of the '68 marathon? "My country did not send me to Mexico City to start the race," he said. "They sent me to finish the race."*

John Wesley was ordained at age twenty four, was an active preacher for sixty five years, and died at age eighty eight. He preached forty two thousand, four hundred sermons (fifteen per week for fifty four years), traveled two hundred and ninety thousand miles, mostly on foot or horseback, and then died leaving a worn out coat, a battered hat, a humble cottage, a tattered bible, and the Methodist Church. The revival he brought to England probably prevented a revolution similar to the one in France. In order to accomplish all this, Wesley died to himself daily and lived for Christ and other people.

Success is not a destination but a process and the process requires discipline. We tend to want our dreams and visions to become a destination where we can simply arrive.

We dream of a career, education, or relationship which we make a destination. If we only get there, we will achieve happiness. But do not focus on standing on the winner's podium; focus on running the race.

Life change is a process. Success is a process! Failure is a process! No single event changes lives. It is the decision made that changes lives. Then, begins the daily activity of running the race. A successful life is a journey of successes.

Our race is to realize God's Plan for our life, our destiny. Realizing His plan is not just knowing and understanding it. Realizing His plan is to reach for it and work at it. Realizing is not just a cognitive exercise; it is fulfilling His call on our lives. It is to understand what part of the great commission we are to fulfill and do it. The Apostle Paul used the example of a race in much of his writings.

> *1 Corinthians 9:24-27 (NKJV) Do you not know that those who run in a race all run, but one receives the prize? Run in such a way that you may obtain it. And everyone who competes for the prize is temperate in all things. Now they do it to obtain a perishable crown, but we for an imperishable crown. Therefore I run thus: not with uncertainty. Thus I fight: not as one who beats the air. But I discipline my body and bring it into subjection, lest, when I have preached to others, I myself should become disqualified.*

Paul provides us with four elements of the disciplined life.

1. Start Running.

Many people want to study about running and talk about running, but never run. Do you want to love God? Fall down on your knees and start worshipping Him.

Do you want to learn to pray? Start praying. Do you want to love your neighbor? Start loving him. Do you want to feed the poor, heal the sick, cast out demons, and raise the dead? Just start doing it.

Goal setting is important, but goal doing is more important. You are more apt to act yourself into feeling, than feel yourself into acting. We often want to feel it first. Procrastination is caused by our perception that doing something will cause us pain. Fear of failure, fear of success, difficulty of the task, and monotony all challenge us to be disciplined.

2.   Desire Excellence.

Run in such a way as to win the prize. For many, including many Christians, mediocrity is the goal. Most people today have an attitude of only doing enough to get by. We learn that from elementary school on through university. Some schools have even done away with grading systems because they do not want a child to be hurt if someone else is better. Excellence is a choice. Mediocrity is over rated. Pay attention to detail. This is discipline. Set high standards for yourself.

We are mediocre, not because of talent, conditions, bad luck, background, or personality. We are mediocre because of choice.

3.   Maintain an Eternal Perspective.

Paul tells us we run for an imperishable crown and eternal reward.[142] Problems will arise as we move toward our destiny.

---

[142] 1 Corinthians 9:25

The enemy will attack, and we will become discouraged as difficulties arise. Nehemiah faced this dilemma in restoring the walls of Jerusalem. Sanballat, Nehemiah's political opponent and governor of Samaria, kept ridiculing him and demoralizing the workers with threats. In addition, Tobiah, the governor of Ammon, threatened to attack with Sanballat. As a result, the people lost sight of their purpose and became discouraged. Nehemiah reminded the leaders and the rest of the people that they served a great and awesome God.[143]

4.   Have faith

Faith is not just believing in something. Faith puts action to the belief. You may believe that a high wire artist can push a wheel barrow across Niagara Falls on a cable, but faith is getting in the wheelbarrow and riding across the falls. Chapter 11 of the Epistle to the Hebrews cites several great examples of some Old Testament heroes of the faith.

By faith Abraham obeyed when he was called to go out to the place which he would receive as an inheritance. And he went out, not knowing where he was going. He did not know where he was going, but he knew Who he was going with.[144] Abraham's faith was less than perfect. Abraham first went half way to the place God called him to go, and only eventually, did he obey completely.

Yet thousands of years later, God does not "remember" the delayed obedience, only the faith.[145] Others with faith are

---

[143] Nehemiah 4:14
[144] Hebrews 11:8
[145] Acts 7:2-4

mentioned in this chapter of Hebrews, and then Chapter 12 explains:

> *Hebrews 12:1-3 (MSG)* [1] *Do you see what this means —*
> *all these pioneers who blazed the way, all these veterans*
> *cheering us on? It means we'd better get on with it. Strip*
> *down, start running — and never quit! No extra spiritual fat,*
> *no parasitic sins.* [2] *Keep your eyes on Jesus, who both began*
> *and finished this race we're in. Study how he did it. Because*
> *he never lost sight of where he was headed — that*
> *exhilarating finish in and with God — he could put up with*
> *anything along the way: cross, shame, whatever. And now*
> *he's there, in the place of honor, right alongside God.*
> [3] *When you find yourselves flagging in your faith, go over*
> *that story again, item by item, that long litany of hostility*
> *He plowed through. That will shoot adrenaline into your*
> *souls!*

Strip down and get serious about achieving your destiny. Get rid of those things which detract you and let Jesus be your example. Jesus never lost sight of where He was headed. We should never lose sight of our vision and passion which will fuel our discipline and lead us to our destiny.

The greatness of what Nehemiah was doing kept him on track.

> *Neh. 6:3 so I sent messengers to them with this reply: "I*
> *am carrying on a great project and cannot go down. Why*
> *should the work stop while I leave it and go down to you?"*

Columbus wrote in his diary, over and over again. "Today we sailed on." "Today we sailed on." *Why?*

He had a vision and a passion; that is what kept him on course. If Columbus said it, we should also say it.

19. Goals

As Army ROTC cadets at Georgia Tech, we were required to attend a Leadership Training Course at Fort Gordon, near Augusta, Georgia. These four weeks provided intense classroom and field training. The field training simulated actual combat situations. One dark, moonless night, our unit was divided into groups of three, taken out into the deep, overgrown woods, and instructed to find our way to a rendezvous point some three miles away. We were lost and had no idea where we were. And more, we had never been to the rendezvous site. We were handed a compass, a white handkerchief, and a terrain map. The map had an "X" designating our drop off point and a "Y", the rendezvous point. This was before Global Positioning Satellites, cell phones and hand held navigation devices.

"I can't say I was ever lost, but I was bewildered once for three days." Daniel Boone

Our mission was to find our way through the woods, underbrush, and swamp, without the aid of a light, to our goal where we would meet up with the other teams. Did I say it was a dark, moonless night? Before we were dropped off, we were able to look at the map and find the range and bearing to the rendezvous point. For us it was two miles Southwest, or 225° on the compass. It would be hard on the team who came in last. It was similar to the television show, "The Great Race," but was many years before the show appeared.

Earlier that day we had practiced night vision in a lightless "Dark Room." One of the most amazing things about our eyes is their incredible dynamic range. We can see in very bright sunlight, and we can also see in nearly total darkness.

New digital cameras seem to have the ability to amplify or attenuate light so the picture becomes clear. The range that our eyes have comes from three different parts of the eye: pupil, rods, and cones.

In biological night vision, molecules of Rhodopsin in the rods of the eye undergo a change in shape as they absorb light. Rhodopsin is the chemical that allows night-vision, and is extremely sensitive to light. Exposed to a spectrum of light, the pigment immediately bleaches, and it takes about thirty minutes to regenerate fully, but most of the adaption occurs within the first five or ten minutes in the dark. Rhodopsin in the human rods is less sensitive to the longer red wavelengths of light, so traditionally many people use red light to help preserve night vision as it only slowly depletes the eye's rhodopsin stores in the rods and instead is viewed by the cones. [146]

After our eyes adjusted to the darkness, with the compass we determined the direction we were to head. Walking straight was impossible due to the trees and underbrush. So we sent one person ahead with the white handkerchief as a marker. In the almost total darkness we could see the handkerchief about fifteen to thirty feet ahead. With the compass the handkerchief was positioned in line with our final destination. The handkerchief became our near term goal on our way to the final rendezvous.

This Army training taught me several things about setting goals.

---

[146] http://en.wikipedia.org/wiki/Night_vision

1. Before you set any goals, you have to know where you want to end up.
2. Before you set your goals, you have to know where you are right now.
3. When you set a goal, it must be in alignment with your ultimate destination.
4. Even though you may not be able to see the ultimate destination, you have to be able to see the goal from where you are today.
5. The path to your goal may be fraught with hidden perils: swamps, forests, and angry dogs,
6. You must keep your goal in sight and be unwavering in your quest.
7. You must take the first step toward your intermediate goal. When Joshua arrived at the Jordan River prepared to take the people into the Promised Land, the river was at flood stage. He could see the other side, but before him lay a formidable challenge.

Joshua 3:7 (NKJV) ⁷ And the LORD said to Joshua, "This day I will begin to exalt you in the sight of all Israel, that they may know that, as I was with Moses, so I will be with you."

Joshua called the leaders together and told them to prepare to cross the Jordan.

Joshua 3:13 (NKJV) ¹³ And it shall come to pass, as soon as the soles of the feet of the priests who bear the ark of the LORD, the Lord of all the earth, shall rest in the waters of the Jordan, that the waters of the Jordan shall be cut off, the waters that come down from upstream, and they shall stand as a heap.

As soon as the priests stepped into the water, the river dried up and it was safe for everyone to cross. But the river did not stop until the people took the first step. When you have reached your intermediate goal, you must then set your next goal toward the realization of your destiny.

"Keep your goals out of reach, but not out of sight,"
(John Maxwell)

When the Lord first called me into full time Christian ministry, we realized there were several things which needed to be considered before that could happen. First and foremost was family. Would my wife agree? Actually, it was not being in ministry full time that held her back from agreeing. Many people we knew were entering seminary and being ordained. She wanted to be sure that I was not just jumping into something because everyone else was doing it. Another issue was financial. With a daughter in college and a son in a private Christian high school, how could we afford to continue financially? Our situation was solid now, but ministry earnings would fall dreadfully short of my executive compensation in an international corporation. Our life style, while not extravagant, did reflect a comfortable standard of living. It seemed our life was like a merry-go-round that kept going faster and faster. Could we get off? Did we want to get off? Would we be hurt if we jumped off? These are the things that kept bothering us over the next few years as we continued to pray.

Over the next two years a series of events occurred which reawakened our dream. Two close friends decided to leave their positions at Boeing Aircraft Company to enter a partnership in an engineering firm in suburban Seattle. They happened to remark that it would be good if I could join them. We thought about this for a long time.

Then our daughter Rhonda got married with only two semesters left in college. She went on to graduate, but she and her husband Rick picked up their own expenses. Our son Kevin graduated from high school and decided to move back to Mississippi to attend college.

In my business profession two incidents arose: a senior position was coming open in the Department of Defense and I was asked to consider it. In another situation, the International Space Station design program had begun and I was asked to consider being on the design team.

Then on a business trip to Seattle, Rita and I had dinner with friends Larry and Audrey Eddings, the leaders of Wind of the Spirit Ministries, an international ministry based in the area. They said that if we moved to Seattle, they wanted us to be involved in their ministry. We explained that we were still waiting for a clear direction from the Lord to either stay in San Diego or move to the Seattle area. Larry told us something momentous, "I have found that when there is no clear direction from the Lord, we have a choice and He will bless whatever we choose."

That settled it; we would move to the Pacific Northwest. I called my friends who had invited me to join them. They asked me to come and meet with the other partners. The meeting went great and we went back to San Diego to await a formal offer. That was early December. In April we still had not heard from them. When queried, they said that they were working on an offer and would get back to me.

On April 20, Rita accompanied me on a business trip to Oakland. After the completion of the business, we drove out to the Napa Valley to have dinner.

During the meal we talked about our future and being in ministry. A week before, I had a dream where we sold our house, gave up the ministry we had established in Southern California, and without any job, moved to Seattle. We would jump off that merry-go-round and seek a new direction in our life. When I shared the dream, Rita became excited and agreed that was the answer. We were tired of waiting. It was time to get on with God's call on our lives.

We returned to San Diego on Friday and called our friend who was a real estate broker and put our house on the market. Our rendezvous point was to be in full time ministry. The first goal was to leave the expensive San Diego and move to a more reasonable Pacific Northwest.

On Monday, after writing my resignation letter to my boss in Washington DC giving him forty five days notice, I informed my immediate staff of my decision. That afternoon a letter arrived from the partnership in Seattle. They offered me a position, apologized for the delay and hoped I would not be offended by their meager salary offer. Earlier Rita and I had estimated what it would take for us to get by after making the move. The offer we received was exactly the amount we felt we could live on. The next day a national Christian renewal organization called. We had been associated with them for several years and they knew we were considering a move. The executive director asked where we were on our move. When I told him we had just made the decision to move and would be there by July, he asked me to consider becoming their Western Regional Overseer. It would not be a salaried position, but I would be able to raise support.

After making our decision to take the first step to our long term goal, things began to fall into place. We left a lucrative position in San Diego and received a position that would support our physical needs while we began a new ministry with two different, non-conflicting, renewal organizations.

If you performed the exercises in the earlier chapter of this book, you should have a good idea of who you are and why you are where you are and where you are going. You have the terrain map in front of you and you can visualize the direction you need to head in order to reach the rendezvous point, your destiny. It is important now to begin your progress to your destiny.

Activity

1. What is your first intermediate goal on your way toward your ultimate destiny?

2. What obstacles that must you overcome - finances, family, forest, or flowing water?

3. Which obstacles do you need God to overcome for you?

Focus

Earl Nightingale once reported[147]

> *If you ask one hundred men at age twenty five if they plan to be successful in life most would say, "Yes." Then at the age of sixty five, one will be rich, four will be financially independent, five will still be working and fifty four will be broke."*

Why do they fail? The opposite of courage is not cowardice; it is conformity. That is the trouble today, conformity; everyone acting like everyone else without knowing why nor where they are going. Why do they conform?

They believe their lives are controlled by external forces that they have no control over. This is called "Determinism." Recently the so-called "Occupy" movements exemplified this concept of determinism. People sat down on Wall Street in New York and at city halls and state capitols around the nation. If you asked them why they were protesting, most did not even know. They just were dissatisfied with their lives and did not see any hope. So they blamed it on someone else: someone who had become successful.

To them it is a "Zero Sum Game." A zero-sum game is a situation in which one participant's gain (or loss) is exactly balanced by the losses (or gains) of the other participant. If the total gains of the participants are added up and the total

---

[147] Nightinggale, Earl, *The Strangest Secret*, Ophelia Madison Press, Hagerstown MD

losses are subtracted, they will sum to zero. It is as if there is only one cake and if I eat more than my share someone else will suffer.

If everyone eats only their own portion, everyone gets an equal amount. It is as if there is only so much success in the world and if someone has some that means that someone else has to suffer. But that is not the way it is either in the kingdom of God or in the world of economics. Anyone can achieve their destiny.

You have written a statement of your destiny. You believe you now know what God created you to become. You must now discipline yourself to pursue your destiny. Success is the progressive realization of a worthy ideal. If a man is working toward a predetermined goal and knows where he is going, that man is a success. Who succeeds? The man pursuing a worthy ideal who says, "I want to be this," and then begins to work toward that goal is the one who often succeeds.

Success is the school teacher who is teaching school because she has a passion for seeing children grow; the woman who is a wife and mother because that is what she wants; the man who runs the corner gas station because that is what he always wanted to do. Success is anyone who is doing the predetermined job because that is what he deliberately decided to do. But only one out of twenty does that.

Is there a key to success? You will notice that some people just continue to fail, while others continue to succeed. Some fail and then get back up and succeed. Earl Nightingale says it is because of goals. Some have them; some do not. Think of a ship sailing out of a harbor with no destination. The ship will go where ever the winds blow.

The key to success and the key to failure is that we become what we think about.

Marcus Aurelius was the last of the "Five Good Roman Emperors," and ruled from 161 to 180 AD. He was considered one of the most important of the Stoic Philosophers.

> *A man's life is what his thoughts make of it. (Marcus Aurelius)*

> *A man is what he thinks about all day long. (Ralph Waldo Emerson)*

The Bible tells us that we are to be careful about our thought life. In an earlier chapter we learned how to eliminate our mental strongholds which keep us from obedience to Christ.

> *2 Corinthians 10:4-5 (NKJV) ⁴ For the weapons of our warfare are not carnal but mighty in God for pulling down strongholds, ⁵ casting down arguments and every high thing that exalts itself against the knowledge of God, bringing every thought into captivity to the obedience of Christ,*

We become what we think about. If a farmer plants a field with corn, he will have a great crop of corn in the fall. If he plants weeds in the field, when fall comes he will have nothing but weeds. We are like the farmer and our minds are like the fields. What we plant in our minds is what we will eventually harvest. We will reap what we have sown.

> *Mark 11:23 (NKJV) ²³ For assuredly, I say to you, whoever says to this mountain, "Be removed and be cast into the sea," and does not doubt in his heart, but believes that those things he says will be done, he will*

have whatever he says.

Our mind does not care what we plant; it will return anything we want to plant. Our mind is free. For every action there is an equal and opposite reaction, and we are

the sum total of all our thoughts. We are guided by our minds. A huge earth moving machine has only a tiny driver. Our mind is the tiny driver.

The strangest secret in the world, according to Earl Nightingale, is that we become what we focus our attention on. If we focus on our fears, we will never be able to get out of bed in the morning, but when our minds are full of our goals and purpose we arise excited anticipating the new day.

Nightingale[148] identifies three steps to changing your life:

1. Write down what you want more than anything else.

2. Stop thinking about what you fear.

3. Your success will always be measured by the quality and quantity of the service you render.

If you want to fulfill your destiny, focus on your goals, stop focusing on your fears, and take the next right step toward your destiny.

It is helpful to write down your goals and future so you

---

[148] ibid

will be reminded to think about them. Put a "Post It" note on your mirror to look at every morning. Think about your destiny every day. Understand that you become what think about.

> *Philippians 4:8 (NKJV)* *8* *Finally, brethren, whatever things are true, whatever things are noble, whatever things are just, whatever things are pure, whatever things are lovely, whatever things are of good report, if there is any virtue and if there is anything praiseworthy--meditate on these things.*

Do not worry about how you will accomplish this goal. Leave that to God. Think about your destiny.

> *Matthew 7:7-8 (NKJV) Ask, and it will be given to you; seek, and you will find; knock, and it will be opened to you. For everyone who asks receives, and he who seeks finds, and to him who knocks it will be opened.*

Cut loose of what holds you back. Be free to imagine what God can do through you. All you need is to have a purpose and faith.

> *Act as if it is impossible to fail. (Dorthea Brand in Wake Up and Live.)*

> **Mark 11:23 (NKJV)** *23* *For assuredly, I say to you, whoever says to this mountain, "Be removed and be cast into the sea," and does not doubt in his heart, but believes that those things he says will be done, he will have whatever he says.*

Fear will cause you to fail. Doubt in the heart will ruin your opportunities to be effective in following Jesus and realizing the promises of God.

Interstate Highway H-3 opened on December 12, 1997 after twenty years of technical, environmental, and political problems. The highway connects the naval base at Pearl Harbor with the Naval Air Station in Kaneohe on the North Shore. The Highway tunnels through the Ko'olau Mountains exiting several hundred feet above the Haiku Valley on a viaduct down to the Likelike Highway. In 1991 it became my task as an electronics engineer to investigate the highway

contractor's concerns about radiation from the Coast Guard navigational system antenna which threatened equipment and workers.

The first afternoon on site was spent surveying the task. Only one lane of the viaduct was under construction and looked like a giant diving board extending about two hundred feet out from the mountain side and about two hundred feet above the valley floor. My job was to move out to the end of the last segment of the viaduct and make measurements. I began to panic. My fear of heights and my fear of bridges caused me to shudder just thinking about spending all of the next day on the end of the pirate's plank.

I drove to the site praying after an anxious night with little sleep. Nearing the construction zone, it seemed the Lord was reassuring me, "Keep your eyes focused on your work and not the danger around you."

Going out to the end of the viaduct and returning to the mountain was scary; however, all that day, as I focused on my work, my fears totally disappeared. When taking a break I was even able to enjoy the awesome view of Kaneohe Bay with the ocean beyond and the lush jungle greenery of the Haiku Valley below.

Our doubts are traitors, and make us lose the good
we oft might win by fearing to attempt.   (Willlam

Shakespeare)

Dr. Norman Vincent Peale wrote

This is one of the greatest laws of the universe…my greatest discovery outside of my relationship with God; if you think in negative terms you will get negative results, if you think in positive terms you will get positive results. Believe and succeed.

Galatians 6:7 (NKJV) Do not be deceived, God is not mocked; for whatever a man sows, that he will also reap.

Do these three things: think about where you are heading; do not think about the things you fear; and do the things that will move you forward towards your destiny. Then you will be well on the road to living up to your potential and becoming the person God created you to be.

If you have enjoyed this book and would like to recommend it to others the author would appreciate it if you would write a review on Amazo.com. The link for a giving a review is below.

https://www.amazon.com/review/create-review/ref=cm_cr_dp_d_wr_but_top?ie=UTF8&channel=gl ance-detail&asin=B00KCRGBWC#

Thank you,

Bill F. Johnson

Realizing Your God-Given Purpose -

Small Group Resource:

14 sessions of interaction.

Each CD contains Teachers Manual, printable student manual and PowerPoint presentations.

Available only from Aslan Press at:

http://www.aslanpress.com/small-group-resources.html

ABOUT THE AUTHOR

William F (Bill) Johnson is an award winning writer specializing in the fields of Christian leadership and discipleship. In the early 1980's Bill left his successful career as an executive in the aerospace/electronics industry to use his gifts and talents in service to the Lord. He continued part time as an engineering consultant as a means of financing his seminary training and ministry activities serving as Regional Overseer for a national renewal ministry, and a church consultant. He then became a pastor, church planter, and mentor to pastors and leaders. In 2001, Bill and his wife Rita founded Aslan Ministries, a non-profit ministry devoted to encouraging and equipping the church and its leaders to fulfill their God-given destiny. Together they have developed and taught dozens of classes and workshops in discipleship, leadership, and ministry. They have traveled extensively teaching throughout the US and several foreign countries.

Other Books by William F. Johnson

All are available at Amazon, Barnes and Noble, and http://www.aslanpress.com.

Motivation, Your Guide To Fitting In; Aslan Press 2014

Leading Your Ministry to Financial Health; Aslan Press 2014

Physician, Heal Thyself, The Oxygen Mask Principle; Aslan Press 2015

Dis-Organize or Bust; Aslan Press 2016

Pray Like Jesus; Aslan Press 2017

Built to Last; Aslan Press 2018

Heal Like Jesus Aslan Press 2019

Made in the USA
Middletown, DE
01 June 2019